Sony Pictures
Animation

Presents

The Art of

SMURFS™

THE LOST VILLAGE

The Art of
SMURFS
THE LOST VILLAGE

Foreword by VÉRONIQUE CULLIFORD

Written by TRACEY MILLER-ZARNEKE

Book design *by* IAIN R. MORRIS & BARBARA GENETIN

TITAN
BOOKS
LONDON

CONTENTS

FOREWORD
BY VÉRONIQUE CULLIFORD

A ll my life, I have been surrounded by the magic of blue creatures, kind of heart but small in stature—they measure three apples high, to be figuratively exact. These creatures leapt into existence from my father's imagination: Pierrot "Peyo" Culliford first shared "Schtroumpfs" with the world in *Spirou* #1071, published in Belgium on October 23, 1958, and pure joy has come from their presence ever since.

In comics, toys, television, and film animation, the Smurfs (English for "Schtroumpfs") have charmed several generations of children and adults, and it is with great happiness that I have watched the story of *Smurfs: The Lost Village* come together now at Sony Pictures. Peyo was always very interested in technological advances and, had he been alive today, I am sure he would have been excitedly involved in the process of making this film and taking the story of the Smurfs in a fun new direction. He always enjoyed seeing his characters evolve, and his passion for cinema would have grown deeply by being a part of the work we do today.

I am most appreciative of the artistic crew at Sony Pictures Animation for taking great care in opening the next chapter of the Smurfs story, realizing it the way I know my father would have been proud to see. Personally, it is always an honor as much as a duty to carry on the legacy of the Smurfs and to protect these characters to make sure they retain their evergreen—or should I say ever-blue?—status, and I am thrilled to have walked this creative path of discovery with such talented filmmakers.

I hope you enjoy experiencing the adventure of *Smurfs: The Lost Village* as much as we enjoyed making it.

PAGE 1: *Gargamel* by Noëlle Triaureau
PAGES 2–3: *Smurfberry harvest* by Kristy Kay
PAGES 4–5: *Forbidden Forest* by Wendell Dalit
PAGE 5, INSET: *Forest adventure* by Joty Lam
ABOVE: *Vitruvian Smurf* by Patrick Maté

ESCAPE EXIT

WATCH TROUGH WINDOW (BROKEN BRANCH)

EXIT   feeding pets

FIREFLY

CAMOUFLAGE

NEST

Alarm

ABOVE: *Color key* by Dean Gordon BELOW: *Smurfy Grove* by Aurora Jimenez

Pillow Plant

A JOURNEY OF DISCOVERY

From humble beginnings as a misspoken word in 1957 to a legacy that extends across more than half a century, the Smurfs are a beloved part of cultures around the globe. Who would imagine that when instead of asking for the salt Peyo muttered something like the word "Schtroumpf," it might evolve into a bit of a game among friends, replacing noun and verb and adjective alike in French . . . and then that word might evolve into an endearing name for magical forest beings, which then translated into English as "Smurfs?"

Pierre "Peyo" Culliford, a cartoonist of Belgian descent, was influenced by the Marcinelle School of illustration and fell in line with artists who drew more cartoonish than anatomically correct proportions. A true fan of cinema, Peyo was particularly fond of then contemporary Walt Disney films. Peyo's comic work was featured in such well-known Belgian publications as the newspaper *Le Soir* and the magazine *Spirou*, and it was during the series for Johan and Peewit that the Smurfs first appeared in 1958 as forest dwellers and the makers of a magical flute. These blue-bodied elfin creatures quickly captured the hearts of many and have been showcased to date in their own comic books, in figurine and toy forms, in a 1976 Belgian animated film, in theme park attractions, in an

American television series, and, most recently, in two previous feature films by Sony Pictures Animation.

With respect to the previous incarnations of the Smurfs, this particular film skips all the way back to the original well of source material to discover its visual inspiration. While translating the 2D world in which Peyo worked into a 3D cinematic experience, director Kelly Asbury remembered the joy he felt looking into a Viewmaster as a child and knew that he wanted to recall the sensory experience of those beautifully crafted 3D sets. "I want people to feel like they are in a world that is magical, an enchanted reality that is oddly miniature, not real but real enough to make our audience want to crawl into this magical place," he explains. Asbury aligned with a literally homegrown artistic leadership team to work with *Smurfs*: both production designer Noëlle Triaureau and character designer Patrick Maté were raised in France and grew up reading the Franco-Belgian comics by Peyo.

Producer Jordan Kerner has a long history with Smurfs as well, having first learned of their existence on a vacation in Hawaii, when friend NBC President Brandon Tartikoff was considering making the books into what would become the 1980's animated television series. "He asked me to read three books, and I instantly fell in love with the world Peyo had created. Brandon and I discussed whether they would best be suited to a Saturday morning treatment or a prime time television treatment. He wanted to keep them just as Peyo created them. So the classic Smurfs, as we know and love them, were beamed into televisions all over the world for Saturday mornings!" Kerner recalls. After decades of studio conversations, the pieces of the feature film puzzle fell

ABOVE: *Rabbit wrangle* by Yuchung Peter Chan

into place at Sony Pictures on a live-action path following Kerner's successful hybrid films, which included *George of the Jungle*, *Inspector Gadget*, and *Charlotte's Web*. . . yet all along he had hoped, one day, to reintroduce audiences to these characters in a modern, spectacular, and fully animated Smurfs movie. President of Sony Pictures Animation Kristine Belson adds, "There's nothing more important in animation than great character design. In our fully animated movie, we pay homage to Peyo's original designs, which are so incredibly pleasing. This new vision combines the best of the classic and contemporary Smurf worlds, and I couldn't be more proud of what Kelly and his team have accomplished."

To ensure that Peyo's vision remains strong in this film, his daughter, Véronique Culliford, was welcomed to give input at every step of the production process. "We have had many long chats about Smurf lore to make sure we are following the thought and design process along Peyo's path. Véronique has even said that if Peyo were alive, he would ask, 'How did you know this is what I had imagined?'" recalls Kerner.

While it is an honorable artistic endeavor to continue the journey that Peyo launched for his Smurfs, this creative adventure has required countless expressions of visual development talent to forge its cinematic path. This book presents just a small peek into the tens of thousands of storyboards, character design, and location concept pieces that were hand-drawn in pencil, lined out in ink, or digitally painted and rendered during the development of *Smurfs: The Lost Village*. Consider it a visual road map on the journey of discovering where Peyo may have imagined his charming blue characters could travel with the team at Sony Pictures Animation.

BACKGROUND: *Dragonfly ditch* by Yuchung Peter Chan and Dean Gordon
ABOVE: *Gutsy Smurf's room* by Yuchung Peter Chan and Karen DeJong
RIGHT: *Buttercup* by Marcelo Vignali and Naveen Selvanathan
OPPOSITE: *Final film frames*

COLORSCRIPT

Production Designer Noëlle Triaureau and her team visually charted the path for *Smurfs: The Lost Village* in the colorscript. This creative roadmap defines many levels of artistic foundation, covering time of day, emotional arcs, and character arcs in both abstract color bars and thumbnail color

ACT 1

0132 WTS	0134 GRC	0330 EXP	0133 EWP	0337 BRD	0635 GML
WHAT IS A SMURF?	GROUCHY'S BENCH	BRAINY'S EXPERIMENT	EVIL WIZARD PLOT	SMURFBOARDING	GARGAMEL'S LAIR

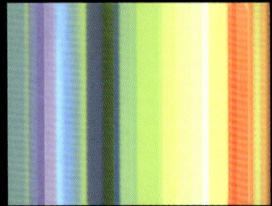   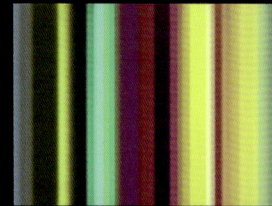 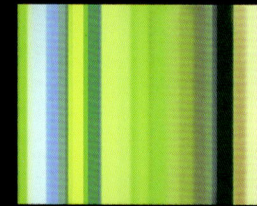 

ACT 2

1737 CMP	1837 RFT	1935 RIV	1937 BCH	1938 CAP	2030 MEG
CAMPFIRE	BUILDING A RAFT	RIVER	BEACH	CAPTURE	MEET THE GIRLS

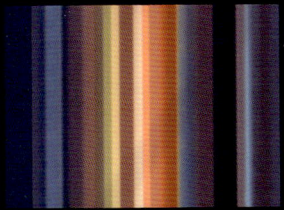 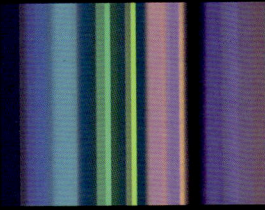   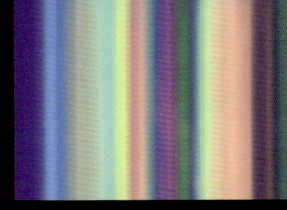 

ACT 2

1030 PUR
GARGAMEL PURSUES THE SMURFS

1335 STN
SMURFENTINE

1430 RBT
RABBIT WARREN

1530 WRG
SMURFETTE WRANGLES BUNNY

1730 MSS
MISSING SMURF

1735 WLK
MOONLIGHT WALK

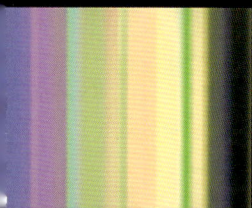

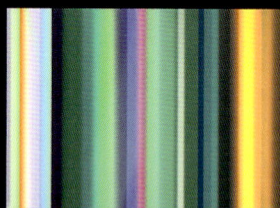

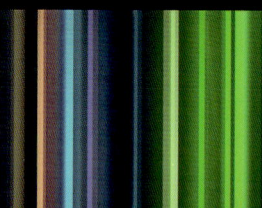

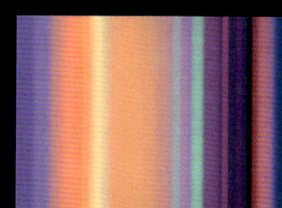

sketches of key moments in each sequence. "This art direction guide is a very informative template for many levels of work that follows," notes visual effects supervisor Mike Ford. The color shorthand language expressed in this tool leads directly to the creation of black-and-white tonal keys for lighting, environmental color exploration, and key lighting frames that inform how lighting should flow for an entire sequence.

30 CHS
OWLIBIRD CHASE

0735 PSD
PAPA SCOLDS THE SMURFS

0837 SNO
SMURFETTE SNEAKS OUT

0530 ENT
ENTERING THE FORBIDDEN FOREST

0935 FLW
SMURF EATING FLOWERS

1330 DFY
DRAGONFLIES

 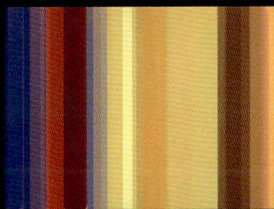 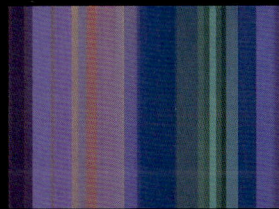  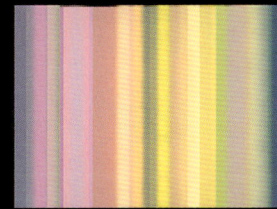 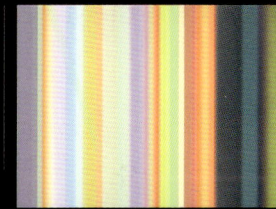

2137 REC	2130 GLG	2133 RTN	2430 PSU	2530 GAA	2535 DW
RECON	GIRL VILLAGE	CLUMSY AND SMURFSTORM RETURN	PAPA SHOWS UP	GARGAMEL ARRIVES	DOWN I THE DUMP

 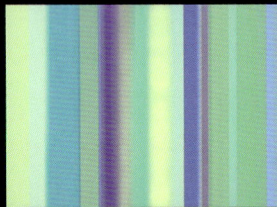  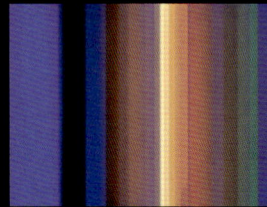  

ACT 3

2635 CAG	2730 VSG	2835 LMP	2520 REV	2935 WRP	3030 END
CAGED SMURFS	SMURFETTE VS. GARGAMEL	LUMP OF CLAY	REVIVING SMURFETTE	WRAP UP	END BUTTON

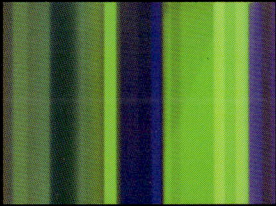 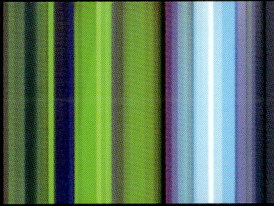 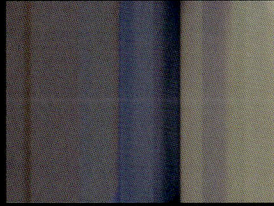  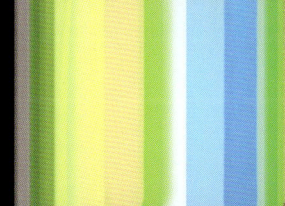 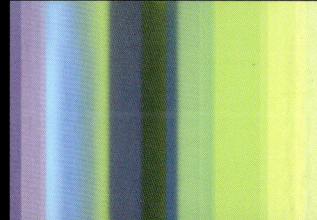

17

-1-

WELCOME TO SMURF VILLAGE

With its warm color palette and soft, rounded shapes, the Smurf Village is an inviting community . . . assuming you can find it. The village does not have a cloaking charm over it: it is simply well camouflaged by nature, accessed only by a certain hollowed-out log. "Once upon a time you would raise a branch to reveal the village, lifting an invisibility shield, but we chose to let nature be the only protection it needs," explains production designer Noëlle Triaureau. Interestingly, Peyo never drew a shot of the entire village in his original comic books, so the artistic team had to conceive that view on its own. "We use over-lapping ground and rolling hills to add depth, and winding paths lead the eye around the village, with lots of S-shapes in branches that compose both foreground and other framing elements," she continues.

The surrounding forest and iconic mushroom-shaped houses reflect the visual language of the Smurfs themselves: they are friendly shapes, always solidly grounded, with rounded corners and smooth edges. The houses echo the shape of a Smurf with a big head/roof and a small body. The mushroom structures are not real mushrooms simply hol-lowed out, but instead they are miniature stucco and wood homes that resemble mushrooms to support the camouflage effect in the forest. "We wanted them to feel tactile and real, so that our audience could imagine themselves entering these magical places," says director Kelly Asbury. The visual lan-guage goes even deeper than the surface, however. "When you think of Smurfs, you think of mushrooms, so throughout the film we have established safe shapes that are stocky and stout, echoing the simplicity of these characters. These serve as a design signal for the audience, so that when we see a stocky and stout shape, it tells us subconsciously that we are safe and can relax," explains art director Marcelo Vignali.

Within their own village, Smurfs build all their own objects, but these objects appear oversized to give a sense that Smurfs are small creatures. For example, utensils are huge, and countertops are high enough to require that Smurfs stand on stools to reach them. Enhancing both the handmade and the small-scale reads is the use of texture on these props. "To make sure objects do not look industrialized, we paint over regular textures or create them from scratch. For example, on metals we use watercolor swatches to create irregularity everywhere within the surface. It is the variation and asymmetry that convey a hand-done quality," says art director Dean Gordon.

PREVIOUS PAGES: *Color key* by Noëlle Triaureau
TOP RIGHT: *Smurf Village invisibility shield*
by Kristy Kay and Naveen Selvanathan
MIDDLE RIGHT: *Smurf Village* by Sean Eckols
RIGHT: *Papa's lab, interior* by John Butiu and Naveen Selvanathan

ABOVE: *Brainy's helmet* by Yuchung Peter Chan and Naveen Selvanathan
RIGHT: *Smurf Village stoplight* by Marcelo Vignali and Wendell Dalit
BELOW: *Blast shield* by Yuchung Peter Chan and Lizzie Nichols

I love how even something as simple as Smurfberry pie can show scale when you look at grains of sugar on it.

— NOËLLE TRIAUREAU,
Production Designer

ABOVE: *Smurfberry pie*
by Marcelo Vignali and Wendell Dalit
TOP RIGHT: *Bunny and carriage* by Patrick Maté
RIGHT AND BELOW: *Food carts and pots*
by Yuchung Peter Chan and Sean Eckols

Crêpes

WAFFLES

SMURF FOREST

We don't try to change what Peyo has done, but rather we try to realize it. We had to make many decisions about the level of texture, detail, and design for translation into CG, but all of these are done with intent to support the comic books, not to modify them.

— MARCELO VIGNALI, Art Director

BELOW AND INSET: *Smurfboarding area* by Aurora Jimenez
BOTTOM: *Smurf Village log entrance* by Marcelo Vignali

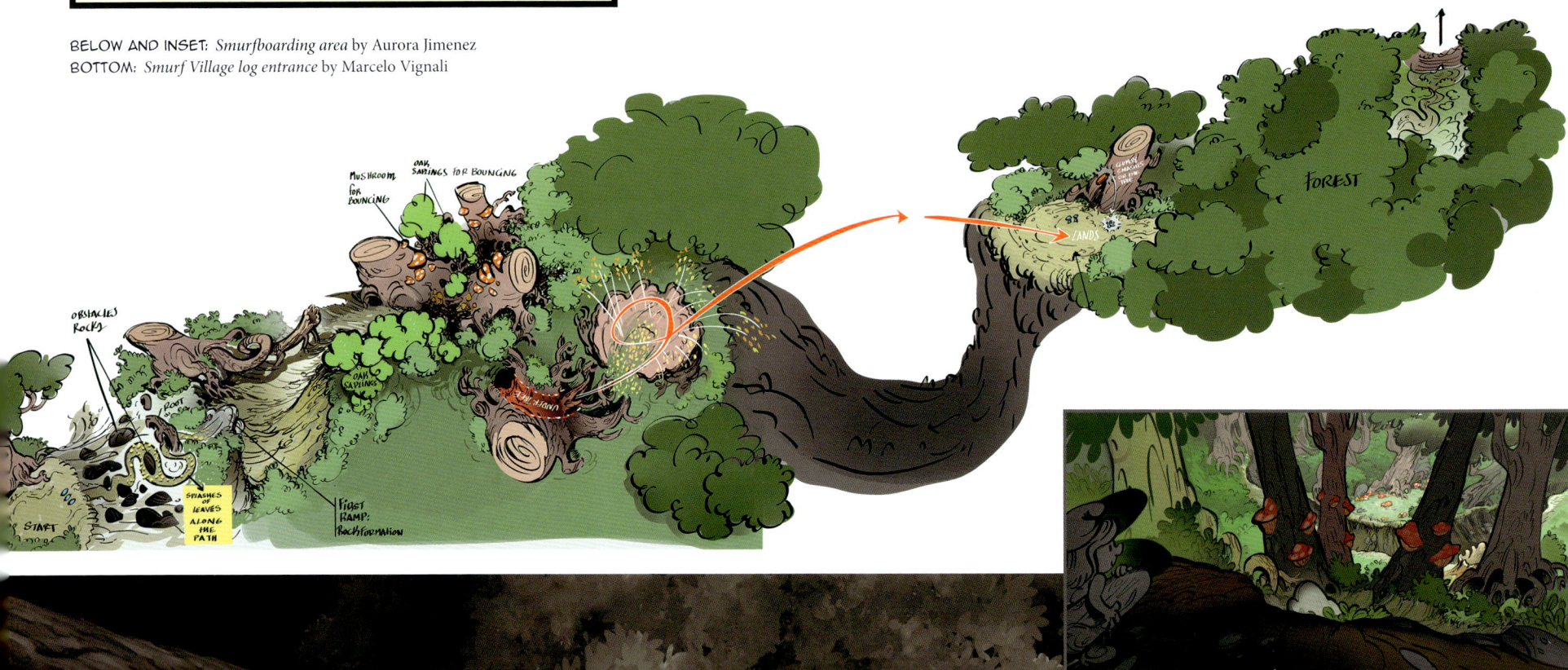

leaves to scale
for sapling

MEET THE SMURFS

Even though the exact genetic composition of Smurfs remains a mystery, one look at this elfin civilization confirms that they are all related. Smurfs can all be described as "young, fresh and fun, with big heads, feet, and hands; small bodies and arms," explains production designer Noëlle Triaureau. Leading the effort to translate Peyo's creations into the CG animation world, character designer Patrick Maté had a fun take on how to whip up a Smurf design: "I look at the Smurf build like a recipe: the head is an egg, a droplet for the body, and beans for their feet." To top it off, the Smurf hat is iconic and inherently European in its shape as well, inspired by the Phrygian cap seen time and again across centuries in European art and recognized as a symbol for liberty and the pursuit of freedom. "The silhouette of a Smurf looks like an interrogation point. For this reason, the feet are never completely flat on the ground. Their legs bend slightly, which makes the Smurf look springy," explains Maté.

As for building a so-called simplified anatomy, it is not always a simple task. When Smurfs stand straight, their limbs appear tubular and smooth like a water hose, with no visual evidence of knees, elbows, neck, and shoulders. However, these anatomical pivot points do exist within the basic rigging structure of these characters. "Oftentimes, creating simpler shapes in CG can be more challenging than realistic deformations. We had to design a new noodle arm system, sculpt additional corrective shapes, and give animation more sculpting controls to shape the hands and feet of the Smurfs to keep their simple design without showing too much of the CG anatomy that we normally try to articulate," recalls character setup lead Brian Cohen. "Smurfs are cartoon characters. They are very elastic," points out Maté.

MIDDLE RIGHT: *How to Smurf a Smurf, Part 1* by Patrick Maté
RIGHT: *Smurfy notes* by Patrick Maté

SILHOUETTE

EGG

DROPLET

BEAN →

SHAPES

LINES AND COLOR

PROPORTIONS

FEET

SMURFS DON'T HAVE SHOULDERS

EVEN WHEN THEY SHRUG...

...EVEN HEFTY

NO SHOULDER

HANDS

DON'T GIVE A HAND A SPATULA SHAPE...

...BUT A GLOVE SHAPE! DO IT BY OVERLAPPING FINGERS

"What is brilliant about Peyo is that he took designs that are the same and put a simple prop or attitude on a character to make them different," explains director Kelly Asbury. In the world of CG animation, reusing the same model is always efficient. However, that was not the focus for the artistic team on this film: instead, they thoughtfully interpreted the 2D drawings into similar yet unique 3D characters that are clearly discernible in their silhouettes, expressions, and motions. One of the greatest challenges in interpreting a Smurf into 3D was developing an appealing frontal view, as the comic never shows them head-on, particularly because the large nose structure would hide the eyes in certain poses. "It's easy to cheat the position of the eyes or shift the nose in 2D, but in 3D we have considerable geometry to manage in a very small space," explains visual effects supervisor Mike Ford.

OPPOSITE TOP AND TOP: *Clumsy Smurf, Brainy Smurf, Hefty Smurf, Smurfette and Papa Smurf* by Patrick Maté
LEFT: *How to Smurf a Smurf, Part 2* by Patrick Maté

THE EYES HAVE IT

The eyes are an important part of capturing the appeal of a Smurf, as Peyo drew them to be connected, which is a difficult task to re-create in a CG model. "We started to build them the way we typically do any two-eyed model, with skin on a nose bridge between them, but noting that the comics were never drawn that way, we really wanted to take it one step further," recalls animation supervisor Alan Hawkins. On the model, Smurf eyes intersect evenly with a straight line down the middle, "but we try to force a curve so that they look like an overlap instead of a straight line, using an invisible shape that pushes one eyeball back so that they appear to connect and still read as two eyes," he explains.

With their blue bodies and blue irises, the Smurfs peer out from eyes that exhibit the balance between looking believable and yet not human. "We achieve that with careful management of the look of each eye in every shot: We need some level of reflection and add shadows on the outside edges to make them feel like 'real' eyes. We don't add a lot of detail to the iris, and we almost always use a specular highlight to add a cartoony look and to make the eyes really pop," says visual effects supervisor Mike Ford. With the connected eye setup, getting the intended read on the pupil may pose a challenge from a shading standpoint. "Depending on the angle and lighting, you get different looks that are harder to read without having a nose bridge in there. By lifting the white part of the eyes, taking away hard edges, and adding occlusion to get a bit of shadow, we can get the read we want, not a distraction," adds Hawkins.

"Matching the CG Smurf eyes to the comics was unconventional work for us, so we had to approach it differently than with other films. We spent a lot of time working with modeling to create the correct topology, and then we modified our eyelid rigging tools to give animation the controls they needed," notes face rigging lead Marc Souliere. The upper eyelids may appear simple in design, but particular aspects of how they are built make them more isolated and in need of attention. "A certain flare makes them more appealing and gives them a subtle eyeliner effect through the play of shadow on a small ledge," says Hawkins.

For added expression options, the Smurfs have floating eyebrows so that in extreme poses they can rise above the edge of the hat, just as Peyo had illustrated in his comics. While this expression is a fun, cartoony push of the anatomy, "there is an invisible surface that eyebrows grow off of, and when they lift high enough, that surface naturally casts an unwanted shadow, so we watch for that and lessen it to keep the read on the face clear," adds Ford. Smurfette also has eyelashes, and the team applied them carefully so that they would not be distracting but rather add to her expression.

TOP: *Brainy Smurf with sextant* by Patrick Maté
TOP RIGHT, MIDDLE RIGHT, AND RIGHT: *Final film frames*
OPPOSITE: *Papa Smurf, final character render*

It's amazing how Peyo established that Smurfs can all come from the same mold, but can be so uniquely defined by personality, profession, and body language.

— NOËLLE TRIAUREAU, Production Designer

Smurf mouths are always round and smooth and are often portrayed on the side of the face in Peyo's drawings, but the head silhouette does not change, no matter how extreme the expression. "The simplicity of Peyo's linework is great, clearly defining silhouettes. The inherent challenge in dimensionalizing it is that it tends to fall apart in certain poses, namely those that are not three-quarter or profile," says Ford. On the CG Smurfs, the typical mouth system had to be reengineered to work on the side of the face. "Its geometry curves backwards in depth in order to make sense to the camera angle while not elongating the jaw. While that sounds like a simple concept on its own, many things need to work together: moving the mouth down to look a certain way and staying low on the face or off to the side while keeping the silhouette nice and smooth is a real challenge, and thankfully our rigging team was up to figuring it all out," notes Hawkins. "We built a system that allowed the animators to slide the mouth around the face while being able to open the jaw and pose expressions to the camera without breaking the iconic round head profile, explains Souliere.

Thanks to Peyo's wife, Nine, helping him sort out color options, Smurfs are definitely blue, but it takes great consideration to lend the right hue and texture to present "Smurf Blue" in CG animation. "Working to create Smurf blue that is true to Peyo was our goal, but to make it work in intricate environments is another level of challenge," says co-producer Mandy Tankenson. For example, the unfortunate effect of a really warm light on a blue surface is that it will look "hideously purple or brown," says Ford. "To solve that issue, we have to light these characters more neutrally, separate from their environments," he explains. Another color challenge arises when shadows appear. "When you render the characters with our physically based system, you get a lot of saturated blue

ABOVE, TOP TO BOTTOM: *Final film frame breakdown: depth, occlusion, texture, final film frame*

ABOVE: *Final film frames*

indirect bounce that tends to go purple in shadowed areas. We worked closely with the shading and rendering team to control this," says CG supervisor Michael Lasker. On a textural level, when translating Peyo's original drawings in a dimensional way, the visual development and production teams were careful that Smurfs did not appear anatomically realistic in a human sense, with muscles, blemishes, or pores visible. "The overall tone and color of the skin are relatively even, but we add subtle detail into specular reflections as well as slight value shifts to imply simple anatomical features. Adding extra detail where we could was very important so that when the characters went into lighting, the shapes wouldn't appear flat and featureless," adds Lasker.

In fact, bringing Smurfs to life in CG often requires some reverse engineering from the technology involved. "CG animation offers such easy complexity in multiples and in design that it's a temptation to achieve those as goals. We found ourselves removing information purposefully to make sure we maintain a certain level of simplicity, to mimic the comic book. Smurfs are so simple without skin texture or distracting weave on their clothing that we needed to show judicious restraint to stay on target," notes art director Marcelo Vignali. Art director Dean Gordon spent a great deal of time and exploration creating fabrics and surfaces that appear on or near Smurfs. "Scale is so important in this world to make sure the Smurfs don't look like humans. For their clothing, all textures needed to be dialed up three or four times to take it off human scale," Gordon adds.

"Figuring out scale in our movie has been paramount to convey the feeling that Smurfs are small," says production designer Noëlle Triaureau. In a fully animated world, coming up with a specific height was somewhat arbitrary, but the artistic team followed the legacy fact that Smurfs are "three apples high." "This is a French expression meaning that they are short fellows and is by no means a precise measurement," she explains. When Smurfs cross through an environment where humans might also have passed, "we place broken-down wagon wheels and other such remnants of human objects in the forest, to show a relative sense of height," explains head of layout Dave Morehead. Smurf stature is also conveyed through camera language. "Instead of shooting from the standard chest height for a human being, we generally place the camera at nose height for a Smurf, which reflects the view Peyo used in the original comics. It makes the audience feel as though they are tilting down slightly, reinforcing the sense that Smurfs are small," continues Morehead. Indeed, it is clearly a big effort to convey smallness.

> *When working in the Smurf's world, you have to constantly come up with ways to remind the audience just how small they are. That's easy to do when you put a Smurf next to something we inherently recognize is bigger, but when it's just them and foliage, you have to reinvent new ways to express scale in visual language.*
>
> — DAVE MOREHEAD,
> Head of Layout

THIS PAGE: *Forbidden Forest, grouping, night* by Wendell Dalit

SMURFETTE

Peyo's comics reveal that Smurfette is different from other Smurfs, beyond being a female. Crafted by Gargamel out of clay, she was sent in to infiltrate and help him capture the other Smurfs, but luckily Papa Smurf nullified her innate evilness with Smurf magic and welcomed her to join the Smurf community instead. The other thing that is different about her is that her name does not define her, as it does the other Smurfs—Clumsy Smurf is clumsy, Baker Smurf bakes—but what is her purpose or talent? Such is her quest, to discover the answer to that very question in this film.

"Smurfette is having a bit of an identity crisis here. Not only is she an adoptee, but she has also arrived at that age where she wants to find her purpose in life, and no matter how much love and support she feels in this community, she cannot find the answer to this question in this space," explains director Kelly Asbury. That she is a girl who has been told just to "be a girl" is a complicated, confusing place for her to exist and an interesting character arc to complete, as suggested by writer Pam Ribon. At one point in her story, "her struggle becomes 'am I just destined to be what Gargamel made me to be?'—which has a strong emotional ring to it and drives her even more passionately to find her greater purpose," says head of story Brandon Jeffords.

Many iterations of the story reel were cut together in order to establish what Smurfette's struggle was—some with more visuals than exposition, some with Smurfette narrating, and some with Papa Smurf telling her tale. "We had versions that involved a forlorn Smurfette wandering through the village watching everyone else 'do their thing.' There was a version where Smurfette tried to help other Smurfs and failed at each task. In fact, the moment that still exists with Baker Smurf was part of a much larger sequence where her disastrous attempt at baking a cake was the culmination of multiple unfortunate attempts at finding her niche," recalls editor Bret Marnell.

To discover her greater purpose, Smurfette feels compelled to look beyond the safety of her village. In doing that, the story team "had to find right balance of Smurfette being headstrong about venturing out and defying Papa's rules about not going into the forest. We did not want her to come off as

TOP RIGHT: *Character poses of Smurfette* by Patrick Maté
RIGHT: *Unwelcome in Gargamel's den* by Patrick Maté

32

During a high-stakes sequence for Smurfette, scenes are packed with the kind of real emotion that you often don't find in an animated family film, but it is exactly what makes the eventual conclusion so powerful and rewarding.

— BRET MARNELL, Editor

TOP: *Smurfette on a baby Howlibird* by Patrick Maté
ABOVE: *Character study of Smurfette* by Patrick Maté
RIGHT: *Smurfette* by Patrick Maté, Omar Smith, and Noëlle Triaureau

rebellious, but instead as searching for truth," adds Asbury. Thus she and her closest Smurfy friends embark on a journey of discovery not dangerous or scary, but more adventurous and intriguing, along the lines of the classic film *Stand by Me*. "We made sure to age the Smurfs up a bit to seem like young adults going out on an adventure, so that they have wherewithal within the world to take on such a journey," says co-producer Mary Ellen Bauder.

From a visual perspective, Smurfette's signature color is yellow, which is inspired by both her iconic blonde hair and her typically cheerful outlook. "Yellow happens to be a primary color, which is typically associated with good guys as well, so this conveys a sense of innate goodness to our audience," explains production designer Noëlle Triaureau. Her hair in itself required plenty of time in the figurative salon chair for modeling and rigging. "We interpreted Peyo's drawings as a flour sack with a flare at the end, a curve that does not break up while she is running, except for a few flyaways," explains visual effects supervisor Mike Ford. It's almost as if she is wearing an invisible hair net, which helps keep her silhouette clean. An amazing feature of her hairstyle is that animators can flip her bangs and part as needed, just as Peyo did, placing it to camera to carve out a more appealing silhouette.

Smurfette's dress is more complicated in its build than the simple frock that it appears to be. Art director Dean Gordon worked with the look development team to create the proper level of detail needed to express scale. "We want to see a pattern on it, so we used fine linen as initial reference on Smurfette's dress, but we scaled and softened the pattern so that it is does not look like she is wearing burlap," he explains. The simulation of her dress had to be managed delicately as well. "Think about what her dress would be from a Smurf's perspective of less than one foot tall: those four inches of fabric cannot move like a flowing Marilyn Monroe dress," adds Ford.

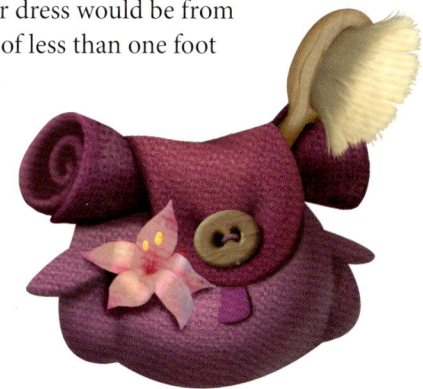

TOP: *Cherry cake disaster* by Patrick Maté
MIDDLE: *Color key* by Yuchung Peter Chan
LEFT: *Smurfette's bedroom* by Yuchung Peter Chan and Naveen Selvanathan
ABOVE: *Smurfette's backpack* by Patrick Maté and Kristy Kay

35

Papa takes Smurfette in, and through a great sense of spirituality on one level and Papa's magic on another, she is imbued with values of the Smurfs and becomes an important member of their community.

— JORDAN KERNER, Producer

TOP LEFT: *Rollerskating* by Patrick Maté
TOP RIGHT: *Final film frame*
FAR RIGHT: *Storyboards* by Erik Wiese
RIGHT: *Smurfette* by Yuchung Peter Chan
ABOVE, TOP: *Color key* by Yuchung Peter Chan
ABOVE: *Color key* by Wendell Dalit

EVIL
SMURFETTE

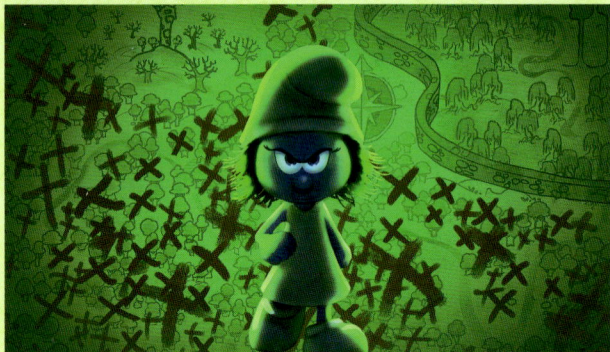

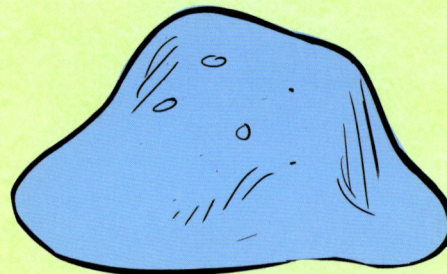

TOP: *Color key* by Wendell Dalit
MIDDLE: *Color key* by Dean Gordon
ABOVE: *Color key* by Jerry Loveland
TOP RIGHT, ABOVE RIGHT, AND BELOW: *Evil Smurfette* by Patrick Maté
MIDDLE RIGHT: *Evil Smurfette* by Wendell Dalit

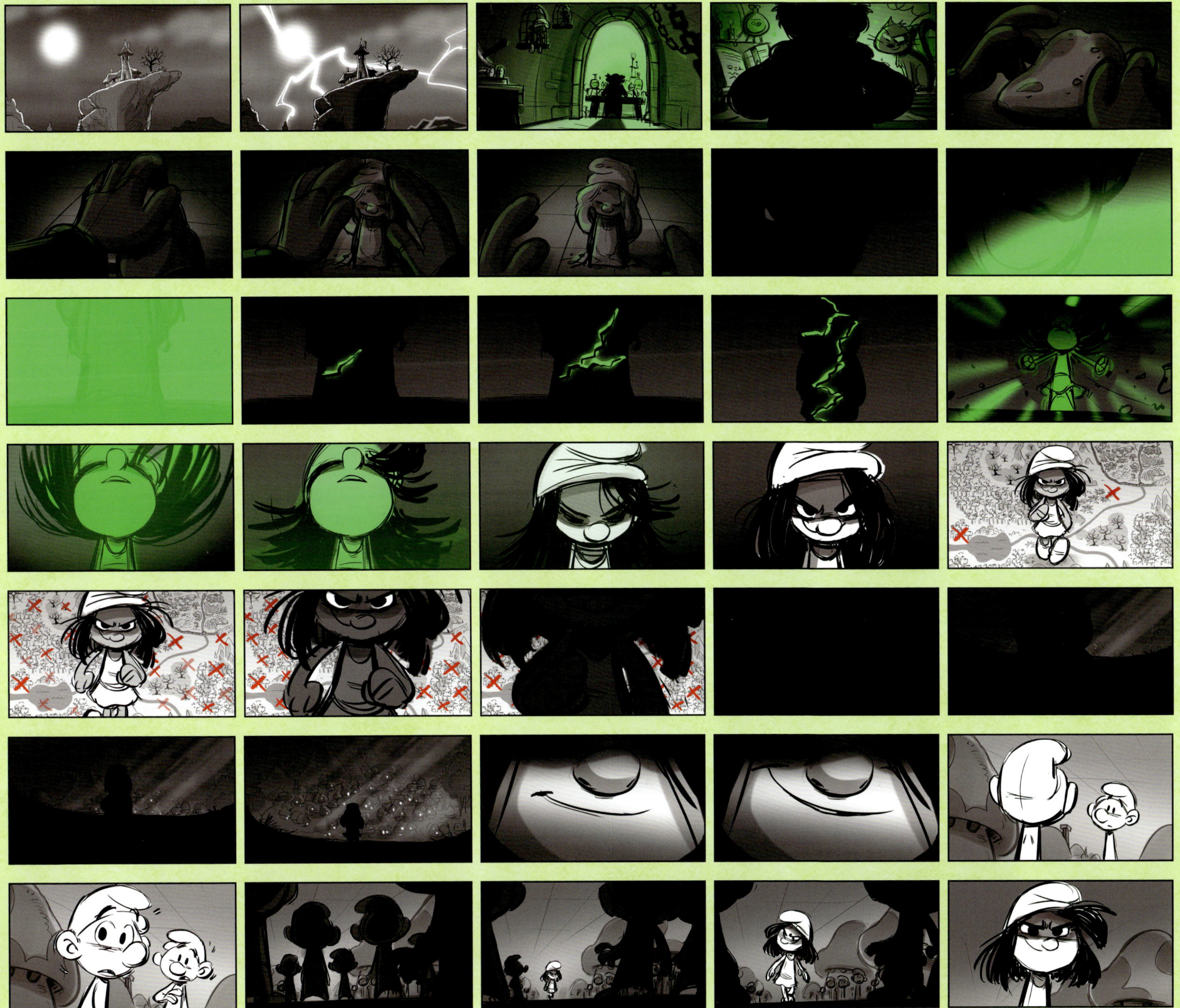

THIS PAGE: *Storyboards* by Jennifer Kluska

CLUMSY SMURF

Clumsy Smurf is exactly what you would imagine: he can't help himself from tripping and falling, but with true Smurf optimism, he does not let that slow him down. In earlier versions of the story, Clumsy was played as more reluctant and fearful over what might happen to him in any moment because of his clumsiness, "but now he is enthusiastic, driven to participate although he just happens to be clumsy along the way," explains animation supervisor Alan Hawkins. Clumsy's posture makes him appear a little smaller than his fellow Smurfs, and his hat sits lower on his head. Perhaps this hat placement is the root cause of his clumsiness, should it fall down over his eyes, but it is certainly a part of the character build that the animation team uses to make him emote. "Even his backpack reflects his personality. It's ripped and patched, as if it's fallen a few times," adds production designer Noëlle Triaureau.

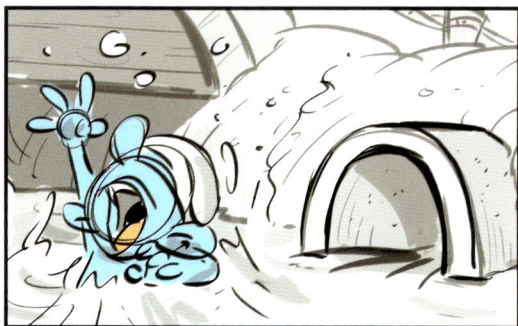

ABOVE: *Storyboard by Steve Fonti*
RIGHT: *Clumsy Smurf character poses by Patrick Maté*
OPPOSITE: *Clumsy Smurf, final character render*

LEFT: *Clumsy Smurf on a baby Howlibird* by Patrick Maté
RIGHT AND OPPOSITE PAGE: *Clumsy Smurf character poses* by Patrick Maté
BELOW: *Clumsy Smurf smurf-boarding* by Marcelo Vignali

ABOVE: *Storyboards* by Jennifer Kluska
LEFT: *Clumsy Smurf with his friends*
Brainy Smurf and Hefty Smurf
by Patrick Maté

BRAINY SMURF

The simple addition of a pair of Smurf glasses with no division in the middle, like a hybrid between goggles and glasses, convinces the audience to believe that Brainy has greater knowledge than the rest of his community. His faster, more staccato cadence makes him seem as if he has so much information in his head that it simply explodes out at every opportunity it gets. "Brainy often corrects others, fiddling with his glasses as a gesture while doing so," says animation supervisor Alan Hawkins. While the glasses are an expressive prop, they require special attention so as not to create unwanted distraction. "We play them pretty clear and not too reflective, often turning down the shadows they create so that they do not complicate Brainy's face," explains visual effects supervisor Mike Ford.

THIS PAGE: *Brainy Smurf character poses* by Patrick Maté
OPPOSITE: *Brainy Smurf, final character render*

ABOVE: *Storyboards* by Casey Lowe

TOP: *Brainy's mobile* by Yuchung Peter Chan and Naveen Selvanathan
BELOW: *Brainy's room* by Yuchung Peter Chan and Wendell Dalit

SNAPPY BUG

One of the smallest creatures in the film, Snappy Bug serves double duty as both a character and a prop. "Snappy Bug brings smartphone abilities to this world, in a super cute and appropriate way," says animation supervisor Alan Hawkins. This simple character is capable of serving as a dictation device, playing back recordings through the fluttering of her wings. She can also re-create pictures by stepping in mud to print them out in little pitter-patter footsteps, not unlike a dot-matrix printer, but obviously in a much more charming way than those desktop machines would.

ABOVE LEFT: *Snappy Bug* by Patrick Maté and Naveen Selvanathan
LEFT: *Snappy Bug, final character render*
FAR LEFT, ABOVE, AND BELOW: *Snappy Bug* by Patrick Maté

ABOVE: *Storyboards* by Brandon Jeffords

47

HEFTY SMURF

Carrying himself like a gym rat, Hefty exudes a sense of strength. "His rig is a little different from the neck down, with his Smurfy teardrop shape almost reversed so that he is barrel-chested," explains animation supervisor Alan Hawkins. He may be well muscled—in as simple of an anatomical portrayal as possible, to stay within the standard Smurf physique—but he is gentle, protective, and kind, literally wearing his heart on what would be his sleeve, if Smurfs wore shirts. "At one point in the production, his heart tattoo was allowed to shift its placement on his arms, to adjust to camera just to keep ingrained in the audience's mind which Smurf this was," recalls production designer Noëlle Triaureau. In the end, his strong presence spoke for itself, without having to rely on that cinematic trick as the 2D cartoons once did.

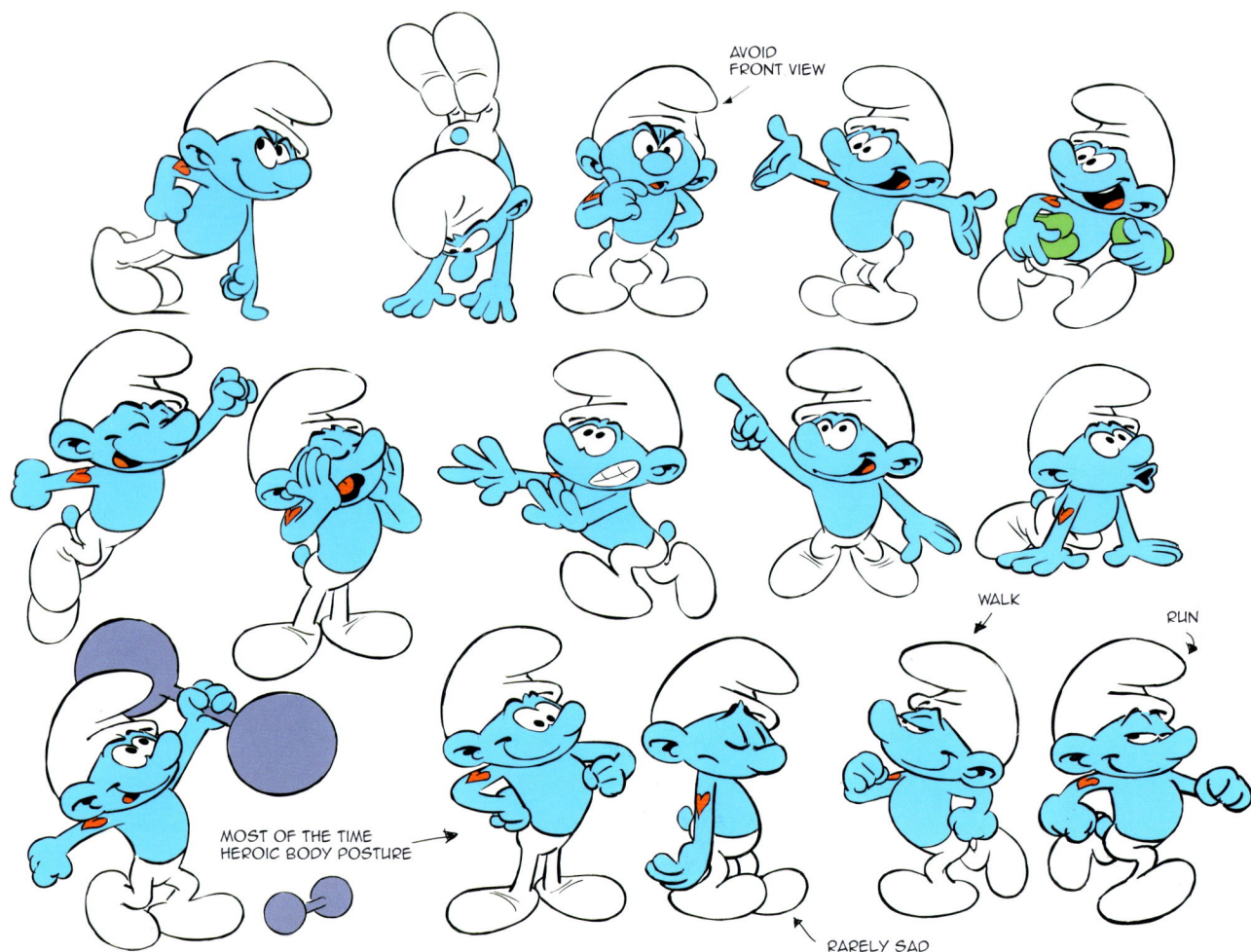

AVOID FRONT VIEW

MOST OF THE TIME HEROIC BODY POSTURE

WALK

RUN

RARELY SAD

For Hefty, his anatomy is slightly adjusted from the other Smurfs. His puffed-up posture makes him who he is more than anything.

— PATRICK MATÉ, Character Designer

TOP AND LEFT: *Hefty Smurf character poses* by Patrick Maté
FAR LEFT: *Color key* by Dean Gordon

LEFT: *Hefty Smurf,
final character render*
RIGHT AND BELOW:
*Hefty Smurf character
poses* by Patrick Maté

PAPA SMURF

Serving as the patriarch of the Smurfs in terms of age and wisdom, Papa Smurf is recognizable by his white hair and red clothing. "Papa has a handlebar mustache contained in an oval-shaped beard," says character designer Patrick Maté. His facial rig is different from other Smurfs since he sports a mustache and beard. "Papa's beard and mustache are the defining elements of his character, but having a lush yet stylized beard on top of a really cartoony mouth is hard to manage, as we don't want to see it stretch with his broad expressions," notes visual effects supervisor Mike Ford.

While his role in this film is relatively small (and not just in stature), his well-established history and authority in the Smurf legacy are what make him the perfect perspective to frame the story told in *Smurfs: The Lost Village*. Papa Smurf stands true as the voice of reason and concern for his youthful counterparts, maintaining a calm demeanor even when some of his community members go beyond their established boundaries. Perhaps that is because he was young once, as explored in an earlier version of this film where Papa was portrayed as young Pieter the mushroom farmer, who endured great tragedy in his past. "That got to be a pretty dramatic and complicated story, which felt too far away from the innocent, simple fun we all love about the Smurfs," recalls director Kelly Asbury. "Anytime we tried to do things that were more serious and involved, it felt like we were wedging sensibility into the story that was just not as entertaining."

Whatever drama Papa Smurf may or may not have encountered in his past, his current existence in the Smurf community is greatly revered.

TOP: *Papa Smurf sketches* by Patrick Maté
MIDDLE: *Papa Smurf character explorations* by Patrick Maté
RIGHT: *Storyboards* by Steve Fonti

Smurfs are both hard and easy to draw—if you can draw one, you can draw them all, as they all have nearly the same silhouette. Differentiating them is a challenge, but small posture cues and accessories help.

— BRANDON JEFFORDS, Head of Story

RIGHT: *Papa Smurf, final character render*

51

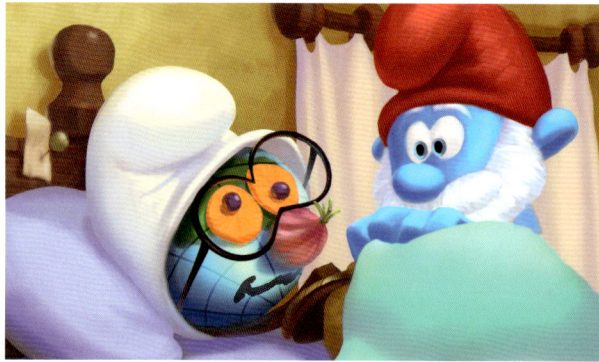

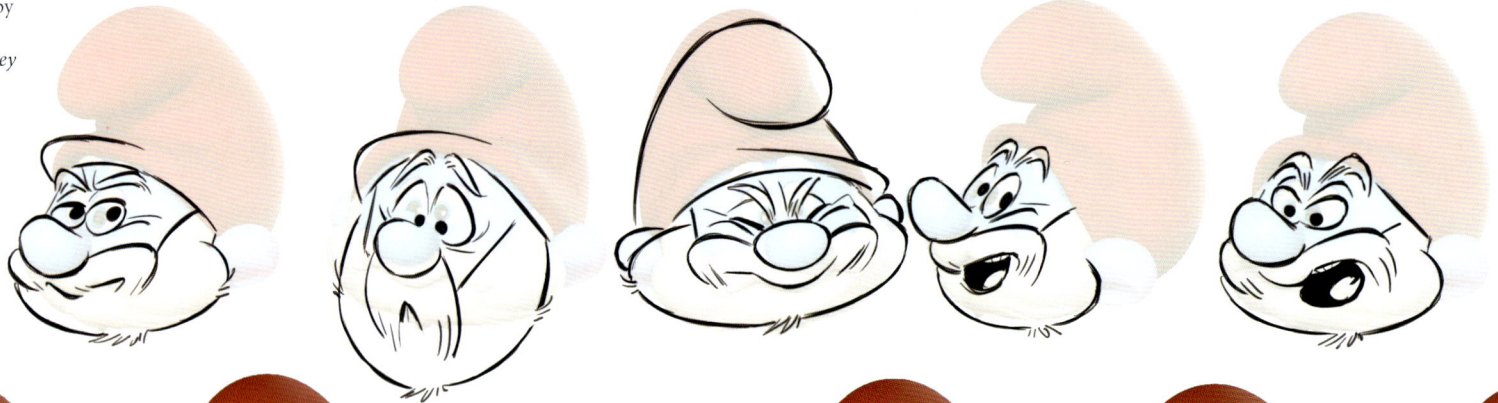

We really wanted a smile crease line for
our Smurfs, but in CG, the mouth doesn't
want to do that on its own. It was great
to see Patrick Maté's initial expression
drawings turned into a template of shapes
that our animators could use to portray
smiles the way Peyo does.

— ALAN HAWKINS,
Animation Supervisor

LEFT: *Forest path to Smurf village*
by Marcelo Vignali and Kristy Kay
ABOVE: *Storyboards* by Denise Koyama

OTHER SMURFY RESIDENTS

Legacy tells us that there are 99 Smurfs in Smurf Village, and many make brief appearances in this film. Some are familiar, such as Baker Smurf, and others are new, such as Conspiracy Smurf. "The looks of certain Smurfs are set in stone, not open to adaptation, and those we create need to remain in that world, without modern-day accessorizing," explains director Kelly Asbury, who was watchful about following the long-established Smurf rules. To round out the cast a bit, character designer Patrick Maté crafted a variety of Smurfs in great detail, but not all of them appear in the final film. "At one point, our story was more about where Smurfs come from, so I had fun exploring how Smurfbabies might be born like peas in a pod, or maybe blossoming from a flower, with a little blueberry on top of their cute little heads," recalls Maté.

What did end up in the film was charming animation, created with the benefit of thousands of poses and face shapes that Maté envisioned. "Even having so many illustrations by Peyo to start with, we need a greater range of motion for animation to work. I had to create images such as U-shapes to show a whistling mouth, for example," he notes. Maté gave animators a lot of information to inspire their work, from attitude to posture to expression. "I wanted to make sure we all worked toward a unifying style of animation, to cover everything about how Smurfs move or talk or come to rest," he adds. But no matter how many Smurfs there are running around, in whatever type of action, "you can never see the top of their heads, even if they take their hats off," says Asbury.

Another aspect of Smurf behavior the film team needed to consider is how they talk, specifically concerning the homage to the origin of the word Schtroumpf/Smurf that Peyo accidentally created and then started to enjoy using in conversation as noun or verb or adjective. "How much we use that language is Kelly's call, but in general we feel that a little goes a long way," explains Kristine Belson, president of Sony Pictures Animation. "I remember when I was growing up with the Smurfs, parents were concerned that it would stop kids from learning how to properly talk and write because they only wanted to use the word *Smurf*," laughs Maté. It's totally smurfable to have those concerns, and clearly the film team smurfed hard to find the right balance in spoken, smurftastic dialogue.

ABOVE, CLOCKWISE: *Smurf characters: Pessimistic Smurf; Clowny Smurf; Baker Smurf and Optimistic Smurf* by Patrick Maté LEFT: *Vanity Smurf* by Joty Lam and Jerry Loveland

KRTZ?

Smurfs have been around as long as I have. We grew up together, except they haven't gotten any older.

— PATRICK MATÉ, Character Designer

TOP LEFT: *Farmer Smurf* by Patrick Maté
ABOVE: *Farmer Smurf* by Joty Lam
TOP RIGHT: *Space Smurf* by Patrick Maté
BELOW: *Checkers pose* by Patrick Maté

THIS PAGE: *Smurf character designs: Fireman, Chimney sweep, Deep sea diver, Karate master, Magician, and Reporter* by Patrick Maté

THIS PAGE: *Smurf character designs: Fireman, Police officer, Miner, Scuba diver, Mime, Handy Smurf, Lumberjack* by Patrick Maté

ABOVE: *Storyboards* by Bryan Andrews

59

THIS PAGE: *Smurf character designs: Parachutist, Fisherman, Sandwich maker, Bungee jumper, Smurf on stilts, Projectionist, Acupuncturist, and Saxophonist* by Patrick Maté

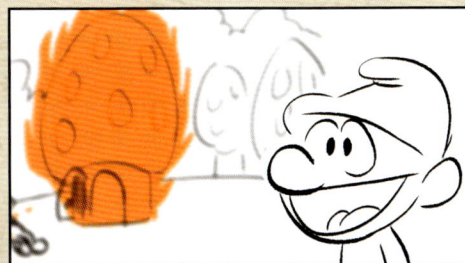

ABOVE: *Storyboards* by Patrick Harpin

ABOVE: *Lazy Smurf studies* by Patrick Maté
BELOW: *Painter Smurf* by Patrick Maté

The real struggle with wanting to tell a Smurfs story is that they are innately innocent characters and we live in a far less innocent time, so the question is how edgy to make the characters to relate to our current culture? The inherent goodness of characters is hugely important to us.

— KRISTINE BELSON, President of Sony Pictures Animation

When we cut from one Smurf to another Smurf and we are in the exact same location, the audience might not notice it's a jump cut. We need to be creative in cuts and make sure shots are completely different—even if we see different accessories, we don't want to confuse the audience into thinking that one Smurf has turned into another.

—BRANDON JEFFORDS, Head of Story

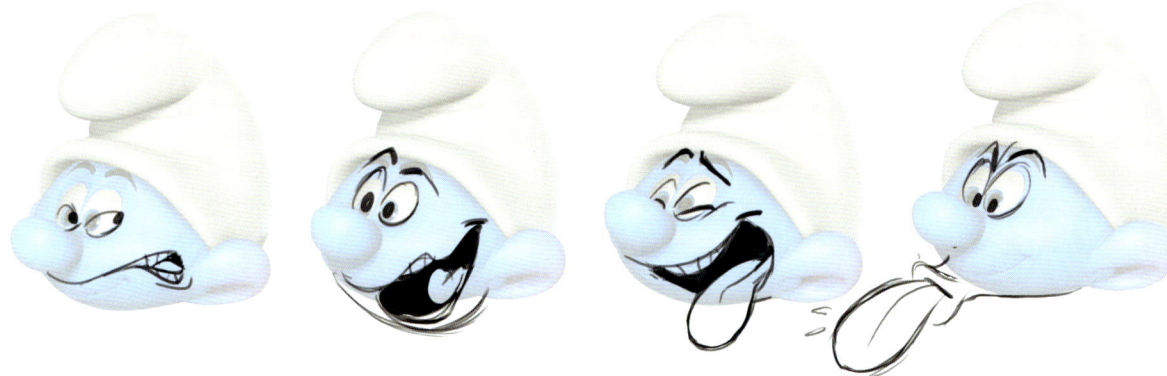

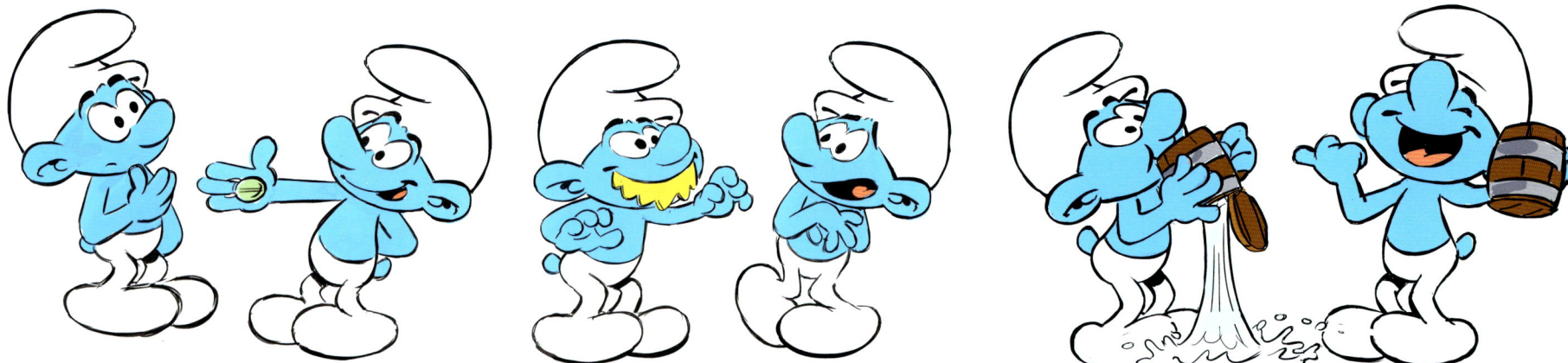

TOP: *Smurfy expressions* by Patrick Maté
ABOVE: *Jokey Smurf character poses* by Patrick Maté

ABOVE: *Jokey Smurf* by Patrick Maté and Wendell Dalit
RIGHT: *Jokey Smurf character poses* by Patrick Maté
FOLLOWING PAGES: *Color key* by Noëlle Triaureau

63

-2-

UNWELCOME TO GARGAMEL'S LAIR

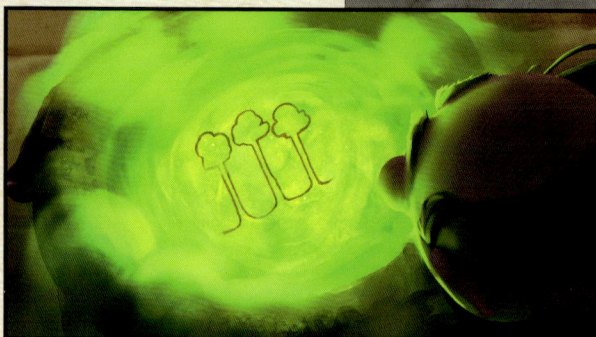

Gargamel's lair is a great contrast to the Smurf Village due to scale, design, and art direction, which combine to create a very different energy and presence. In direct opposition to the lush, grounded green environment of the Smurfs, Gargamel resides in a remote castle seated high upon a rocky crag with a dark sinister cloud directly overhead, firmly stationed there as if in contempt for the otherwise bright blue sky all around it. The artistic team created an unsettling space inside the lair, turning to "dark German expressionism as an influence, using broken cast shadows, angular shapes, twisted perspective, and exaggerated composition," explains production designer Noëlle Triaureau.

Since Gargamel is a human, there is a different treatment of texture in his space due to scale. Elements in his lair have more detail, given that the human scale from a Smurf's point of view really stands out. At the same time, objects need to exist on the same visual playground since the story takes place entirely in the same stylized universe. "Things in Gargamel's world need to look realistic but not photo-real. The art team is great about providing examples of impression, to which the look development team adds material properties for specularity and other levels of CG detail," says visual effects supervisor Mike Ford.

While the color palette in the lair is somewhat playful, it is dramatic due to high contrast, "establishing acidic greens and purples around Gargamel to echo the recurrent visual theme for villains in animation," adds Triaureau. In moments of high action, the greens glow brighter and the shadows grow longer to increase the sense of drama, but the true presence of Gargamel soon becomes clear: a daunting cast shadow of the evil wizard at his cauldron looks absolutely scary until the camera pulls back to reveal a villain who is not exactly what one expects to see.

TOP LEFT: *Storyboard* by Mike Kunkel
LEFT (TOP ROW): *Color key* by Wendell Dalit
LEFT (2ND ROW): *Color key* by Dean Gordon
LEFT (3RD ROW): *Color key* by Wendell Dalit
LEFT (4TH ROW): *Color key* by Wendell Dalit and Noëlle Triaureau
INSETS, ABOVE: *Storyboards* by Paul Watling
RIGHT: *Gargamel's lair* by Michael Spooner

TOP LEFT: *Color key* by Dean Gordon
ABOVE: *Color key* by Jerry Loveland
TOP RIGHT: *Color key* by Wendell Dalit
LEFT: *Gargamel's lair* by Justin K. Thompson and Dean Gordon
BELOW: *Gargamel's lair destroyed* by Aurora Jimenez

ABOVE: *Powerful Wizard's lair* by Yuchung Peter Chan

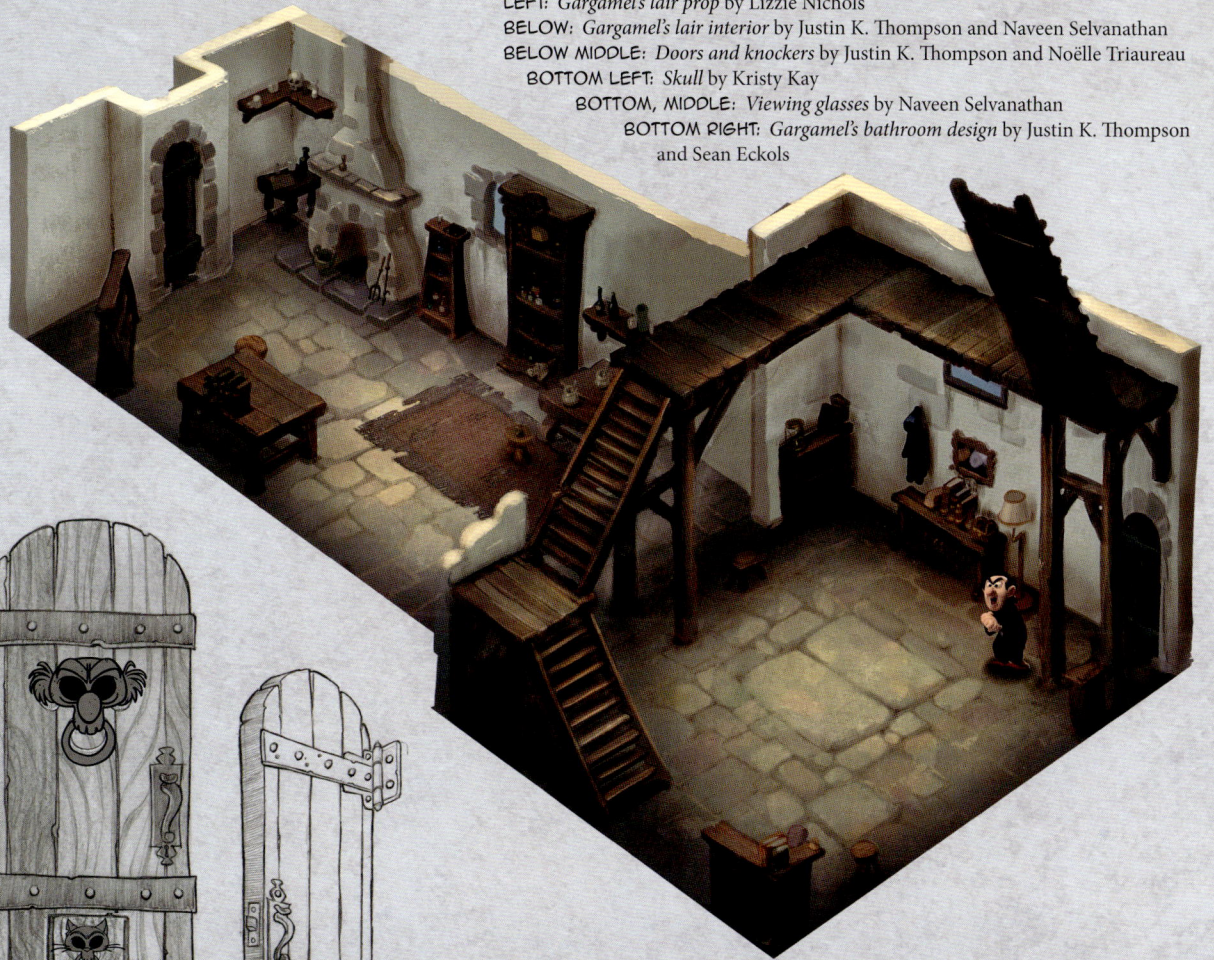

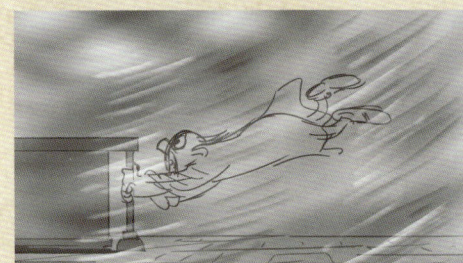

ABOVE: *Storyboards* by Keith Baxter

73

GARGAMEL

Gargamel has the dubious honor of being the only human to appear in the Smurf world portrayed in this film. "He is a wretched guy who thirsts for power and sees himself in lofty terms. He is very operatic in his approach to himself—it's all about him, and he is super greedy. He is everything a good villain should be, but at the same time, he is kind of an idiot," explains director Kelly Asbury. "The portrayal of Gargamel was hard to arrive at, because instinctually we want a villain to be clever, smart, and adept at his villainy. Gargamel is not any of that, neither in tradition nor in design—he's a balding old wretch of a wannabe wizard," adds head of story Brandon Jeffords.

Not that there's anything wrong with thinning hair on top, but in Gargamel's case, his combination of balding pate, goofy expressions, and hunched posture makes him appear to be a bit more of a joke than a threat. To convey a sense of villainy, Gargamel does have evil magical powers, as exhibited by the glowing green "freezeballs" that he uses to capture his prey, and his looming presence is portrayed as exactly such when he is near Smurfs. "To a Smurf, Gargamel is approximately six times as tall, so scenes shot from a Smurf's perspective are threatening," explains head of layout Dave Morehead. Clever, fast-talking dialogue gives Gargamel an air of wicked wit: when he tells his creation Smurfette that she appears to have proven "the rotten apple hasn't fallen too far from the tree," it is not only a scathing blow to her sense of self but also a reference to her diminutive size.

THIS PAGE: *Gargamel character explorations* by Patrick Maté
OPPOSITE: *Gargamel, final character render*

ABOVE: *Storyboards* by Brandon Jeffords

ABOVE AND BELOW: *Gargamel and Azrael character poses* by Patrick Maté

TOP: *Gargamel ancestors character sketches* by Tony Siruno
LEFT: *Gargamel as Powerful Wizard* by Patrick Maté
ABOVE: *Storyboards* by Paul Watling

THIS PAGE: *Argamel, Gargamel's ancestor, character explorations* by Patrick Maté
OPPOSITE: *Azrael and Gargamel poses* by Patrick Maté, models by Omar Smith, Azrael painting by Joty Lam, Gargamel painting by Noëlle Triaureau

It's fun how Gargamel and Azrael kind of treat each other as an old bickering couple, even though Azrael does not speak.

— MARY ELLEN BAUDER,
Co-Producer

AZRAEL

Azrael is Gargamel's long-standing side-cat, an entertainingly cartoony feline who seems smarter than his keeper in certain moments. "They have a strange relationship and don't really seem to like each other. We get the sense that Azrael sees right through Gargamel and knows his act and all his jokes," says director Kelly Asbury. When Gargamel is with Azrael, "we play him flat and very comedic, a cue we learned from the work of the story artists, which we then translate into the DNA of the camera language to convey that these two are funny together, not meant to be cinematic," adds head of layout Dave Morehead.

Azrael is sarcastic and often frustrated with his partner, which he clearly conveys through expressions and paw gestures explored by character designer Patrick Maté. Azrael is partially anthropomorphized, which is to say "he's still very rooted in cat mannerisms but has the freedom to do other humanoid-type things," according to animation supervisor Alan Hawkins. For example, he won't stand up and walk on his hind legs, but he will use his paws to manipulate things and perhaps mimic in a highly entertaining "blah blah blah" gesture with them. Perhaps the most important duty that Azrael fulfills is acting as a sounding board for Gargamel. "Their mostly one-sided conversational dynamic adds to the comedy of the story. Otherwise we'd have a villain who does not interact with others and/or just talks to himself a lot," explains head of story Brandon Jeffords.

As far as design is concerned, Azrael does not stray far from the comic illustrations or what we might expect a real cat to look like, interpreted for a cartoon world. "But instead of having 15 whiskers like a real cat would have, Azrael has only three as a cartoon convention to simplify," explains art director Dean Gordon. His short fur also allows a cleaner silhouette that stays with the action the animators want to portray. "With Azrael's whiskers and some of Gargamel's clumps of hair, we developed a look of thin root to thick tip to emulate the line weight look that Peyo gave his ink drawings," explains production designer Noëlle Triaureau.

The notch out of his ear is the single most important trait that makes Azrael so easy to distinguish from a common cat. It is character design at its best: with the mangled ear, even the mere silhouette of the character tells us who this cat is.

— NOËLLE TRIAUREAU, Production Designer

OPPOSITE, BOTTOM LEFT: *Kitty litter* by Aurora Jimenez and Wendell Dalit
OPPOSITE, TOP AND BOTTOM: *Azrael character poses* by Patrick Maté
OPPOSITE, MIDDLE: *Azrael facial expressions* by Patrick Maté
THIS PAGE: *Azrael, final character render*

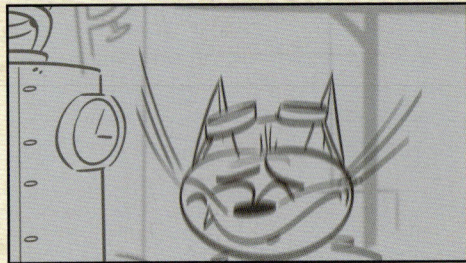

ABOVE: *Storyboards* by Paul Watling

ABOVE: *Azrael character poses* by Patrick Maté
OPPOSITE: *Azrael* by Patrick Maté, model by Omar Smith, painting by Joty Lam

MONTY

Monty is a new addition to the world of Smurfs, although the initial concept for him traces back to the Howlibird of Peyo's creation. The flight path for his development in the film was a long and winding one, because at one point he was a she, he was a griffin, and then "he was a horrible, mean giant bird who lived in his own lair, with the Smurfs only encountering him as they were being sacrificed to him," recalls head of story Brandon Jeffords. That scenario created double villains and was not serving the story well, "but we fell in love with this crazy vulture character that story artist Mike Kunkel brought to life, so we decided we could make him a foil for Azrael. Gargamel seems to think of him as a noble falcon when he's really more like a garbage-eating buzzard. Somehow he is dumber than Gargamel though, so that is good for Gargamel's ego," explains director Kelly Asbury.

Monty's huge eyes are pushed in their design and overlap. He appears dumb and googly-eyed, lacking in co-ordination, "but in other moments those huge eyes combine with his hunter instincts and he can be dangerous and focused," says animation supervisor Alan Hawkins. Perhaps the most impressive anatomy on Monty is his wing system, which grew from years of development in trying to fold a bird's CG wing without causing deformation. To accomplish this complex system, the team had to "loosen the reigns a bit on traditional rigging techniques to be able to achieve these types of comic animation shapes with a highly technical, complicated foundation in the rig," explains lead character setup TD Brian Cohen. The attached feather system alleviated the work of animators having to hand-animate feathers, and the character effects team also gave Monty dynamic feathers to achieve the desired plumage. "We made sure to paint intricacies on Monty's feathers to allow variation, such as the banding detail, which adds design to make them interesting but not busy. A few cuts on their edges communicate featheriness in a stylized way," notes art director Dean Gordon. Iridescence on the black feathers shimmers with a bit of green, echoing the evil color theme established for Gargamel and his Smurf-hunting posse.

84

TOP LEFT AND RIGHT: *Monty flying* by Patrick Maté
RIGHT: *Monty* by Patrick Maté, Dean Gordon, Yuchung Peter Chan, and Noëlle Triaureau
ABOVE: *Baby Howlibirds* by Patrick Maté

ABOVE AND RIGHT: *Monty's character poses* by Patrick Maté
BELOW, LEFT: *Color key* by Wendell Dalit
BELOW, RIGHT: *Color key* by Jerry Loveland and Noëlle Triaureau
BOTTOM LEFT: *Monty* by Patrick Maté and Noëlle Triaureau
BOTTOM RIGHT: *Monty and Gargamel* storyboard by Brandon
Jeffords, draw-over by Patrick Maté

TOP: *Howlibird sketches*
by Patrick Maté
LEFT: *Howlibird babies*
by Mike Kunkel
ABOVE: *Howlibird* by
Patrick Maté and
Dean Gordon
RIGHT: *Howlibird feather*
by Kristy Kay and
Wendell Dalit
OPPOSITE: *Howlibird*
attacks! by Patrick Maté

HUMANKIND LEFT BEHIND

Cut from the film, many other humans once roamed the scenes of *Smurfs: The Lost Village*, including an eclectic band of Vikings who existed within a fairytale-esque Dark Ages version of the Belgian city of Bruges.

Then came a story introducing the ancestors of Gargamel, a popular Renaissance curse shop, and a magical place named Wizard's Peak. "In one story, we played out the idea that Azrael was actually a human turned into a cat, which explained some of his human behaviors and intelligence as a cat, but that never went far," recalls head of story Brandon Jeffords. In another version of that storyline, "this human was a female who had catlike nails, a pointy headdress, and paw-print detail on her gown, which was similar in color to Azrael's fur," recalls art director Dean Gordon.

Other versions featured cameo appearances by Mother Nature, Shakespeare's Nick Bottom, and even Peyo's Johan and Pewitt. Reaching all the way back to the origin of Smurfs, yet another tale involved the magic of a powerful wizard who lived in a grand tree in the center of what would become the Smurf village.

There were versions involving time travel, versions involving anti-Smurf movements, and versions involving pro-Smurf festivals . . . but in the end, spending more time with the humans and all that history meant spending less time with the Smurfs. At last, the decision was made to stay on the course of being true to the source, focusing the story in the world of Smurfs and their never-ending plight called Gargamel.

ABOVE: *Baldrick* by Patrick Maté
BELOW: *Baldrick* by Patrick Maté and Dean Gordon
BOTTOM: *Baldrick* by Patrick Maté and Jerry Loveland
LEFT: *Azraella* by Patrick Maté and Dean Gordon

TOP: *Viking sketches* by Patrick Maté
ABOVE: *Viking* by Patrick Maté
and Wendell Dalit
LEFT: *Gudrick* by Patrick Maté
and Omar Smith
RIGHT: *Viking* by Patrick Maté
and Wendell Dalit

GUDRIK'S

89

Environment is a very big character in this movie, literally and figuratively speaking.

— NOËLLE TRIAUREAU, Production Designer

ABOVE: *Medieval corner shop and street* by Michael Spooner
BELOW: *Solstice Ridge* by Noëlle Triaureau
OPPOSITE, TOP: *Viking camp* by Michael Spooner and Wendell Dalit
OPPOSITE, BOTTOM: *Viking vessel* by Wendell Dalit

TOP: *Bruges canal* by Noëlle Triaureau
and Jerry Loveland
ABOVE: *Bruges signs* by Wendell Dalit
OPPOSITE: *Bruges Townsquare*
by Marcelo Vignali and Naveen Selvanathan

ABOVE AND BELOW: *Wizard sketches* by Patrick Maté
RIGHT: *Wizard's peak* by Dean Gordon

ABOVE: *Wizard's Glade* by Marcelo Vignali
PAGE 96: *Wizard's Glade* by Marcelo Vignali, Joty Lam, and Noëlle Triaureau
PAGE 97: *Forest adventure* by Joty Lam

95

-3-

DISCOVERING THE FORBIDDEN FOREST

As Smurfette seeks the answer to her burning question of "What is my purpose?" she realizes it cannot be found within her village, so she must venture out into the greater forest on a journey of discovery. This is a bit of a risk, because Papa Smurf has long warned his community not to wander too far, not to cross the old stone wall into the Forbidden Forest. When she and her loyal companions make their exit into the woods in the dark of night, it's not really that dark: in order to give a sense of clarity and relative safety in this adventure, "we use day-for-night lighting to keep the sequence light in value as we follow her," says production designer Noëlle Triaureau. This mode of lighting also helps keep the read of blue characters against lush green foliage clearer, a constant challenge for the artistic team.

Slight trepidation arises due to the hikers carrying not just backpacks, but also the weight of Papa's past warnings and the sense of the unknown. Play with shadows and a looming spiderweb above a hole in the stone wall also create a bit of tension, but Smurfette is driven in her effort: she sets her fear aside to lead the group through the wall to the edge of the Forbidden Forest. The visual storytelling goal was to generate suspense, the perfect psychological setup to precede the sense of relief and awe experienced when what lies beyond the great wall is revealed.

PREVIOUS PAGES: *Path to Forbidden Forest* by Noëlle Triaureau
ABOVE: *Bramble patch* by Lizzie Nichols
CENTER, TOP: *Color key* by Dean Gordon
CENTER, MIDDLE: *Final film frame*
CENTER, BOTTOM: *Forbidden Forest* by Dean Gordon
TOP, FAR RIGHT: *Smurfblossom* by Lizzie Nichols
RIGHT: *Path to Forbidden Forest, elevation* by Aurora Jimenez

ELEVATION

PASSAGE THROUGH WALL

DAYLIGHT   LUMINESCENCE

After traversing the dark wall passageway, Smurfette draws back a delicate foliage curtain to reveal breathtaking sunrise light, a time of day that adds radiance and glow to color. This magic light casts the scene in pink values, presenting a lush forest unlike anything the Smurfs—or the audience—have ever seen. Some plant life seems familiar, yet is unique in its color palette. After growing a virtual nursery that features 52 different species of "enchanted" plants, the artistic team designed plant groups with five to seven types per cluster to convey which plants should be placed together so that complementary colors could stay together, avoiding the kaleidoscopic effect of having too many colors at once.

"Making sure these groupings looked good from different angles was essential to keep a certain level of flexibility with layout, story changes, and schedule. Particular attention was given to designing plant mounds with interesting shapes and silhouettes as well as keeping them in an appealing color palette. We never want them to be distracting from our characters, but we do want them to provide a magical feel in this place," says Triaureau. Among the most popular plants are the elephant ear, which can block out bigger areas so the audience can focus on small glowing groups in front of it, and the baby's breath, which works as dots of light that tie a grouping of flowers together like a variegated bouquet.

The trees in this space portray a different look from those that grow in the Smurf Village. Some here feature variegated silver bark, which presents a challenge to get a read as bark instead of the perception of stone. The shape language is a design cue to note as well: "straight, stocky, stout trees grow in the Smurf Village, but twisty, zigzag, spiral-shaped trees grow in this forest," notes art director Marcelo Vignali. Tree canopies are influenced by the shapes Peyo used in his clouds, looking almost "like ice cream scoops, or big simplified shapes with peripheral details of breakup to allow believability," he adds.

Designing groundcover is important, as the diminutive heroes are so close to it. The visual development team harvested its own versions of

TOP AND MIDDLE LEFT: *Hanging bell flower* by Aurora Jimenez
ABOVE LEFT: *Forbidden Forest vegetation silhouette* by Wendell Dalit, Marcelo Vignali, and Noëlle Triaureau
LEFT: *Forbidden Forest* by Yuchung Peter Chan

101

moss and creeping jenny. "We needed to design something that looks nice, where scale reads well and is easy enough for characters to walk through," notes Triaureau. In fact, the characters interact so much with the groundcover that the effects team was brought into the virtual nursery to help solve contact issues, including how much bounce-back the groundcover shows after it has been walked on.

What really makes this environment seem like a Forbidden Forest is the distinctly different flora that blossoms here with huge flowers, magical radiance, and special talents. "The iridescence factor meant having two types of color palettes—one for daylight and the other for the evening or shade—which added an extra level of complexity," explains Triaureau. "Our texture, lookdev, and dev group teams came up with a plant 'look' switcher—if the plant is in shadow, then luminescence in the plant is triggered and it emits a glow from either a light or incandescent textures. If the plant is in sunlight, our standard day-lit textures and shaders are used. It's an amazing mix of artistry and software that saved us a ton of setup time for each shot in the Forbidden Forest," explains visual effects supervisor Mike Ford.

The visual complexity of this world is amazing, but compositionally we always need to know where to look. It's a balance to make such a busy image work around the "egg" of action where you want the audience to focus.

— MIKE FORD, Visual Effects Supervisor

ABOVE: *Forbidden Forest* by Wendell Dalit
RIGHT: *Forbidden Forest modular tree* by Michael Spooner and Lizzie Nichols
INSET, TOP: *Forbidden Forest sketch* by Marcelo Vignali
INSET, BOTTOM: *Forbidden Forest sketch* by Michael Spooner

FORBIDDEN FOREST FLORA

One of the curiously special talents exhibited by a large flower is its ability to swallow up the surprised Smurfs with almost vacuum-like speed, but thankfully the taste of Smurf is not to the liking of these seemingly carnivorous plants. There is also a plant that boldly defends its space with a boxing maneuver. In a much more gentle interaction, yet another plant covers its passersby with kisses. From the bouncing pillow plant to the helicopter flower, visual development artist Wendell Dalit came up with a lot of ideas for how fun and different so many plants could be. "Some plants were built as characters since they need to be rigged to perform. In earlier versions of the story, some even walked or talked," recalls co-producer Mandy Tankenson. One of the once mobile plants is the eyeball plant designed by visual development artist Lizzie Nichols: it has eye-like blossoms to track the action around it and was designed with orchid-like roots that allow it to scuttle along. Even though it remains firmly embedded in the final film, it is still oddly intriguing in its watchfulness.

TOP RIGHT AND BELOW: *Forbidden Forest flora sketches* by Wendell Dalit
RIGHT: *Kissing plant* by Wendell Dalit and Kristy Kay

Ahchoo!

ABOVE: *Angler fish plant* by Wendell Dalit
and Aurora Jimenez
ABOVE, MIDDLE AND RIGHT: *Forbidden
Forest plant explorations* by Wendell Dalit
BELOW: *Boxing plant* by Patrick Maté

*Shapes and color of the Forbidden Forest were designed to contrast
against the regular forest around the mushroom village and to convey
the magical quality of the plants. Also, the terrain of the Forbidden
Forest is much more accidental and without dirt paths.*

— NOËLLE TRIAUREAU, Production Designer

107

OPPOSITE: *Forest vegetation at night*
by Naveen Selvanathan
TOP, MIDDLE, LEFT, AND BELOW:
Eyeball plant explorations by Lizzie Nichols
ABOVE AND TOP RIGHT: *Eyeball plants*
by Lizzie Nichols

OPPOSITE, TOP LEFT: *Enchanted cabbage*
by Lizzie Nichols
OPPOSITE, TOP RIGHT: *Pillow plant* by
Aurora Jimenez and Kristy Kay
OPPOSITE, BOTTOM: *Chinese lanterns* by Yuchung Peter Chan
TOP LEFT: *Mushrooms* by Wendell Dalit
MIDDLE LEFT: *Berry cluster* by Wendell Dalit
LEFT: *Sundew plant (day and night)* by Lizzie Nichols
ABOVE: *Angler fish plant* by Aurora Jimenez

FORBIDDEN FOREST FAUNA

ABOVE: *Bee* by Patrick Maté and Sean Eckols
ABOVE RIGHT AND FAR RIGHT: *Stork poses* by Patrick Maté
ABOVE, MIDDLE: *Stork* by Patrick Maté and Naveen Selvanathan
RIGHT: *Sparrow* by Patrick Maté and Wendell Dalit
BELOW: *Owl* by Patrick Maté
OPPOSITE, TOP LEFT: *Caterpillars* by Patrick Maté
OPPOSITE, TOP MIDDLE: *Frank the caterpillar*, digital render
OPPOSITE, TOP RIGHT: *Steve the butterfly*, digital render
OPPOSITE, BOTTOM LEFT: *Firefly* by Patrick Maté and Sean Eckols
OPPOSITE, BOTTOM RIGHT: *Butterflies* by Patrick Maté

BELOW: *Animal explorations* by Patrick Maté
BOTTOM LEFT: *Snail* by Naveen Selvanathan
and Dean Gordon

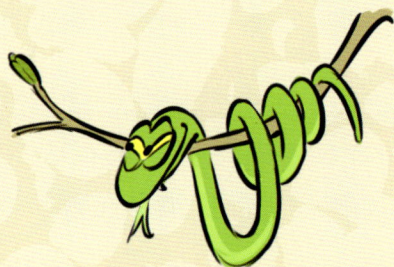

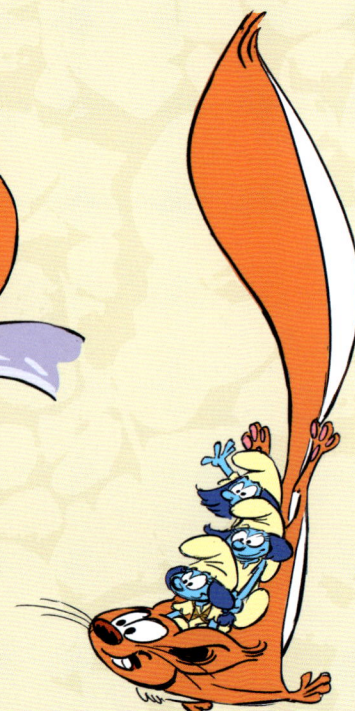

ABOVE LEFT: *Frog and newt explorations* by Patrick Maté
RIGHT: *Newt* by Patrick Maté and Wendell Dalit

DRAGONFLY DITCH

When the Smurfs enter a previously unexplored canyon, they discover yet another fantastically enchanted place. There is softness to the foliage, with weeping willows gracing the top of a canyon, and gently rolling, moss-covered hills down below. "It is aglow with filtered light, and what looks like dancing colorful specks of light sparkling around the cliffs, created as the prism effect of light passing through the wings of the dragonflies that live here," explains production designer Noëlle Triaureau. The dragonfly nests also add color and softness to the setting in their swallow-esque design of round hive-like shapes, constructed out of a rainbow array of dirt and pebbles.

"Early visual development of Dragonfly Ditch made it feel much more foreboding than magical," Triaureau recalls. But luckily light and color prevailed in this environment.

OPPOSITE: *Dragonfly ditch* by Aurora Jimenez, Wendell Dalit, and Noëlle Triaureau
BOTTOM LEFT: *Color key* by Dean Gordon
ABOVE: *Dragonfly nests* by Yuchung Peter Chan and Wendell Dalit
BELOW: *Color key* by Jerry Loveland and Dean Gordon
BOTTOM: *Dragonfly ditch sketches* by Yuchung Peter Chan

117

TOP ROWS: *Dragonflies* by Juston Gordon-Montgomery
ABOVE AND BELOW: *Dragonflies* by Patrick Maté

ABOVE: *Storyboards* by Juston Gordon-Montgomery

DRAGONFLIES

The residents of this canyon are not the typical dragon-flies that come to mind, but are more like actual dragons than anything. "With chubby cheeks and big eyes, the dragonflies are cute but dangerous," points out character designer Patrick Maté. Visual development artist Naveen Selvanathan painted them to have a shiny and translucent quality to make them look like gems when they are curled up. "They are about 75 percent dragon and 25 percent dragonfly, considering their big long tail with spikes, scales, and S-curves," explains animation supervisor Alan Hawkins. They move with a hovering and zippy hummingbird type of action, propelled by an intricate design that involves six limbs and four wings. To create a swarm of these enchanted insects, the modeling and animation teams use a crowd system to alter color, proportion, and size along with flight patterns and angles. "We got our animators warmed up by starting with an assignment of animating a dragonfly cycle to populate the crowd library," adds Hawkins. Speaking of warm, these dragonflies do breathe fire as well, adding to the uncertainty of whether or not they are actually friendly or frightening creatures.

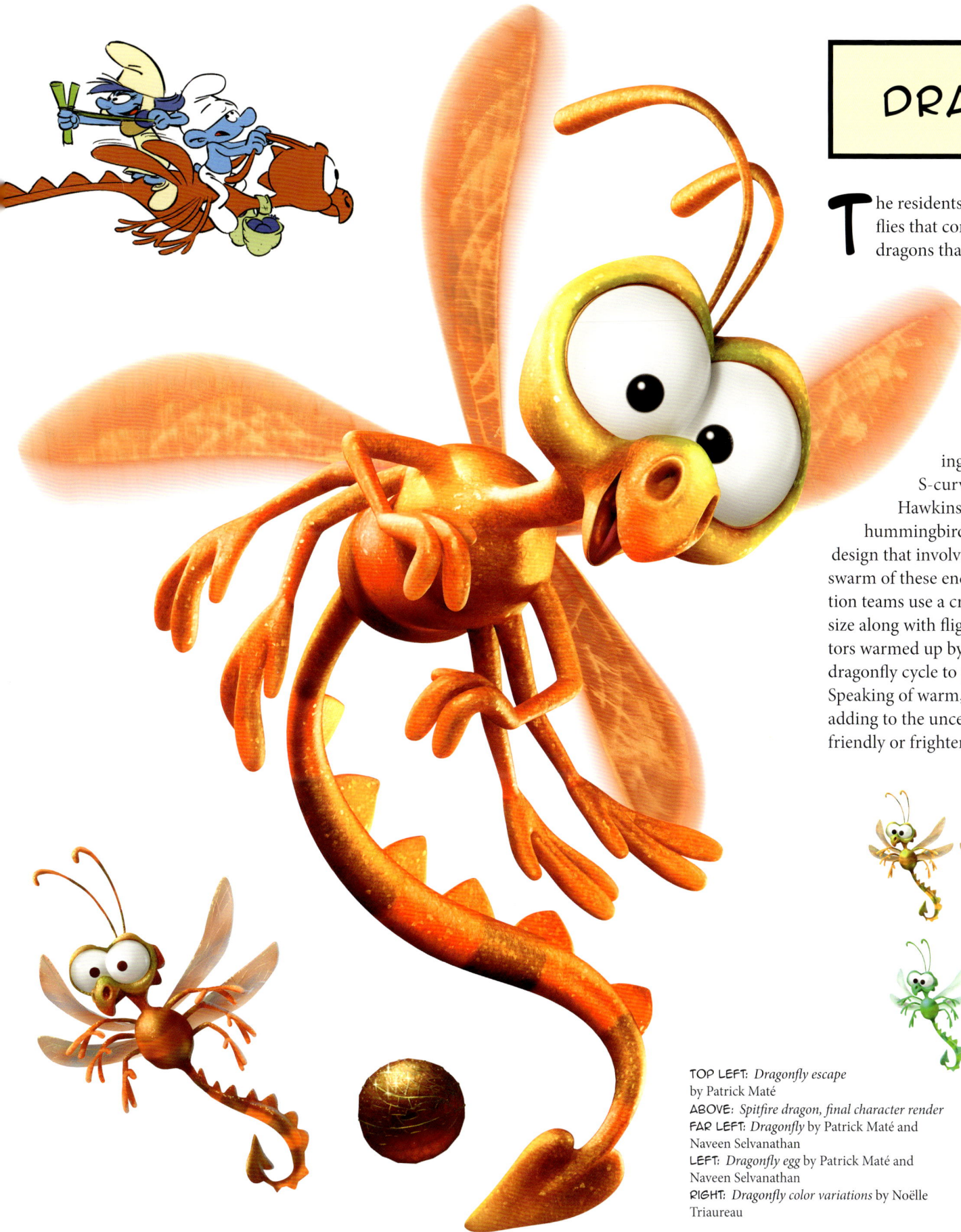

TOP LEFT: *Dragonfly escape* by Patrick Maté
ABOVE: *Spitfire dragon, final character render*
FAR LEFT: *Dragonfly* by Patrick Maté and Naveen Selvanathan
LEFT: *Dragonfly egg* by Patrick Maté and Naveen Selvanathan
RIGHT: *Dragonfly color variations* by Noëlle Triaureau

RABBIT WARRENS

I was lucky enough to meet and learn from Chuck Jones, who taught me that when artists start working on a show, make sure they start on the most fun sequence. By design and a bit of happenstance, the rabbit tunnel sequence is where we started, and it has been a great roller-coaster ride of creativity since story artist Bryan Andrews first boarded it," recalls director Kelly Asbury. The adventure in this space starts with a jump into darkness down separate rabbit holes from the ground level, where the band of trekking Smurfs leap to safety out of Gargamel's chase. "Cinematographically speaking, I love that in CG we could do a transition straight from the ground level where Gargamel gives up the chase into dropping down through the dirt and into the tunnels where the Smurfs have landed," says head of layout Dave Morehead.

Once the focus of the action moves into the darkness of underground, careful camerawork and cutting must continue to convey that each of the four Smurfs is in separate tunnels. "With characters that look like one another at first glance, all in similar backgrounds, it's easy to get confused about who's who and who's where in a bunch of fast cuts. We shot the four tunnels so that the different characters are framed differently, starting from afar and moving into each character in progressive shots," adds Morehead. Each tunnel view features unique shapes in topography designed by visual development artist Aurora Jimenez. There are pointy rocks and roots surrounding Clumsy, the most likely Smurf to get hurt; Smurfette's tunnel shape is elegant and simple; Hefty's is all rocks to echo his physical strength; and Brainy's tunnel is spacious and well lit, as he has a plan for keeping things in control. The different colors of light beams that each Smurf emits from his or her glow bug lamps also help the audience recall which Smurf is which.

Clumsy finally loses control in the darkness of the tunnel and exasperatedly shakes up his energy drink to the point that it explodes. While it is unfortunate that he has wasted his hiking rations, the explosion effects are yet another opportunity to brightly demonstrate Peyo's design influence. "The puffs of dust have a specific profile to match Peyo's style, and the lighting teams created sharp spear shapes that burst out of the explosion to give it a cartoony look," adds visual effects supervisor Mike Ford. Clumsy's action also triggers the entrance of another Forbidden Forest element—the Glow Bunnies.

TOP RIGHT: *Color key* by Kristy Kay
MIDDLE RIGHT: *Color key* by Wendell Dalit
RIGHT: *Color key* by Kristy Kay

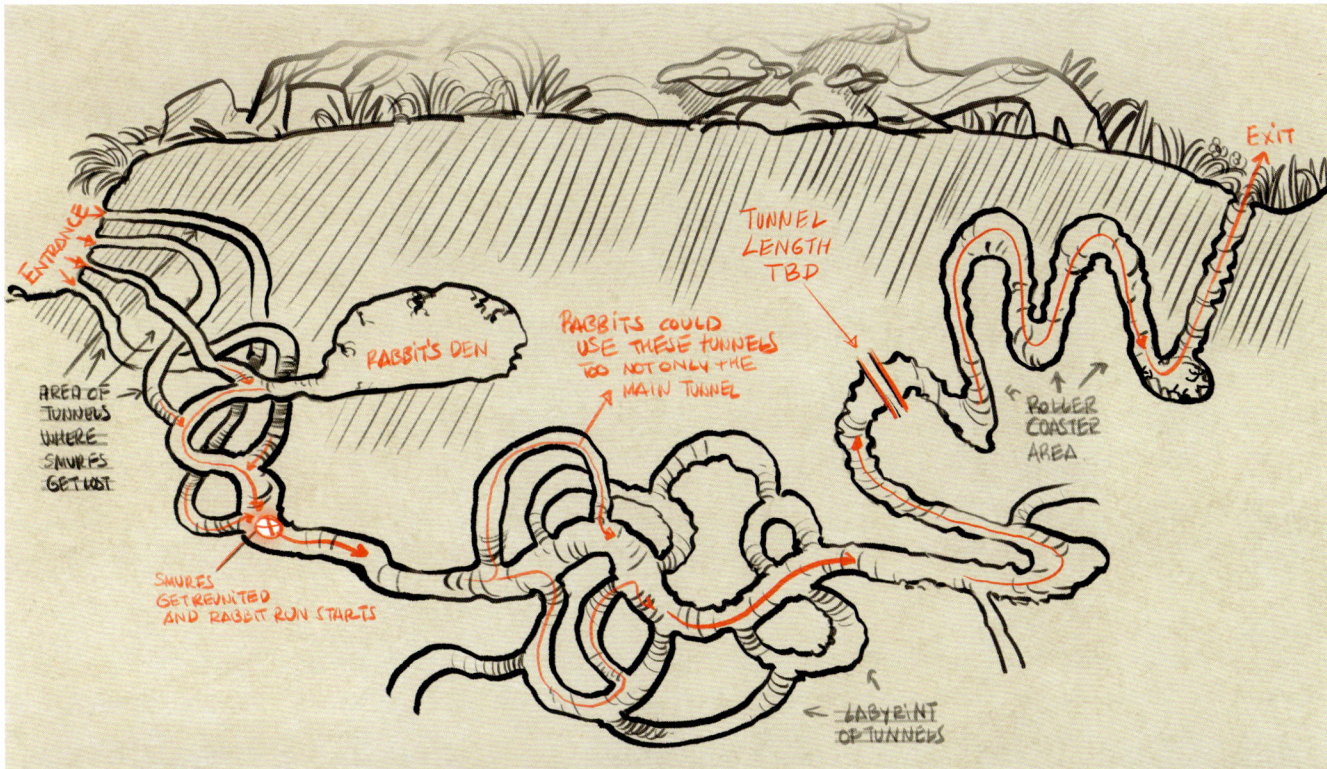

TOP: *Rabbit warren diagram* by Aurora Jimenez
MIDDLE: *Rabbit warren* by Marcelo Vignali
BOTTOM: *Color key* by Kristy Kay and Noëlle Triaureau

ABOVE: *Storyboards* by Bryan Andrews

ABOVE: *Bucky bunny poses* by Patrick Maté
BELOW: *Moonlight walks* by Yuchung Peter Chan
RIGHT: *Discovering the Forbidden Forest* by Noëlle Triaureau
MIDDLE RIGHT: *Color key* by Kristy Kay
BOTTOM RIGHT: *Color key* by Dean Gordon
OPPOSITE, TOP AND BOTTOM LEFT: *Glowing bunny variations* by Noëlle Triaureau, Naveen Selvanathan, and Wendell Dalit
OPPOSITE, BOTTOM RIGHT: *Rabbit eyes* by Lizzie Nichols

GLOW BUNNIES

At first, hundreds of eyes peering out of the darkness of the tunnels seem alarming, but this tension is cut faster than a rabbit can run, as an entire colony of enchanted bunnies makes itself visible. These glow-in-the-dark creatures literally move the action along as they stampede toward the Smurfs, sweeping the Smurfs up onto their furry backs and out of the darkness of the tunnels. At one point in the visual development process, the colony of bunnies exhibited a variety of colors, but they are now all hues of a soft, sandy yellow in daylight, and shades of light green in darkness. They are appealing because of their simplicity, with thoughtful design choices to make them more stylized than anatomical, much like another quadruped in the film. "Just as with Azrael, when their front paws are lifted, they have more of a 'sock-full-of-sand' shape, but when the bunny paws are on the ground, they appear more flat on the bottom," explains animation supervisor Alan Hawkins. No matter how cartoony the shapes, "these characters still need believable fur in order for the audience to connect with them. "For example, the texture has to look fairly naturalistic, and the groom has to follow rabbit anatomy—growing outward from the nose, flowing downward on the leg—even if it glows," explains art director Dean Gordon.

A RIVER RUNS THROUGH IT

Fantastic flora is one element that makes the Forbidden Forest enchanted, but a whole other level of magic exists along the river . . . or, rather, around the river, which contains levitating water, as much as levitating water can be contained. When the story artists came up with this extraordinarily enchanting idea, the production team jumped in headfirst to developing this fun ride. "The rigging team worked with layout to provide 'ribbons' of water to be placed in shots to show flow, at what speed and on what path the water should generally follow," recalls co-producer Mandy Tankenson. Animators take those ribbons and give them movement along with the characters, and then the effects team runs fluid simulation along that path, comparable to running water through a clear tube. "It gets very complicated, with characters and rafts, and then there's the wet cloth, hair, fur, and other elements to consider," notes animation supervisor Alan.

In order to figure out how antigravity water could be portrayed, the effects team found great reference in a video clip of an astronaut wringing out a towel. "The water didn't drop, but instead it coalesced around the towel. Beyond that, we figured out that gravity would be loose around everything that had previously existed in this set, but would still hold pretty true for our characters," explains visual effects supervisor Mike Ford. Once the general flow of water was established, the effects team added in foam elements and turbulence to make it look more realistic, to a point. "With predawn lighting, luminescent plants and splash elements in water that glow like algae, this river environment really fits more into a cartoony world than we normally get to do with water," adds Ford.

The river flows into the downpour of three tall waterfalls. These waterfalls are a key story point, but were much smaller in their earliest concepts. "We had to make them more epic once they became the capper to the levitating river, as it would be too much of a letdown if these were only five or six feet tall," recalls art director Marcelo Vignali. If these are epic on a human scale to the audience, imagine what they must be from the diminutive Smurf perspective.

LEFT: *Enchanted river* by Noëlle Triaureau
INSET: *Levitating rapids* by Marcelo Vignali
ABOVE: *Enchanted river* by Jerry Loveland

125

TOP: *Enchanted river rapids* by Marcelo Vignali ABOVE: *Enchanted river rapids* by Aurora Jimenez

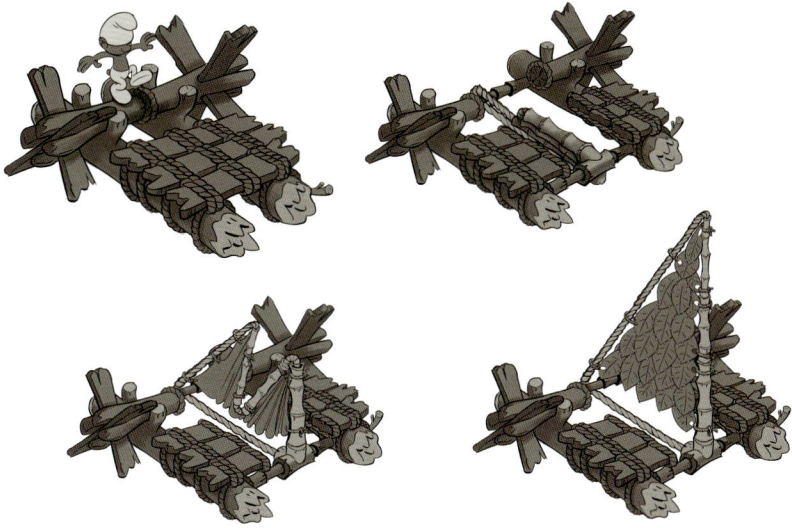

ABOVE: *Unfolding raft* by Justin K. Thompson

TOP RIGHT: *Enchanted river* by Marcelo Vignali and Noëlle Triaureau
ABOVE: *Enchanted river rapids* by Marcelo Vignali

127

TOP LEFT: *Three waterfalls* by Aurora Jimenez and Dean Gordon
TOP RIGHT: *Three waterfalls* by Noëlle Triaureau
LEFT: *Forbidden Forest campsite* by Michael Spooner and Wendell Dalit
OPPOSITE: *Waterfalls* by Aurora Jimenez

THE SWAMP OF NO RETURN

Unlike most features of the Forbidden Forest, the Swamp of No Return is a bit dangerous, as suggested by its acidic green hues. Considering the sickly looking trees that surround it, it is not a healthy environment: production designer Noëlle Triaureau describes it as a "fetid, greenish swamp with geysers spewing out mustard-color fumaroles." Dead logs pepper the landscape, and some even resembled alligators in earlier design concepts.

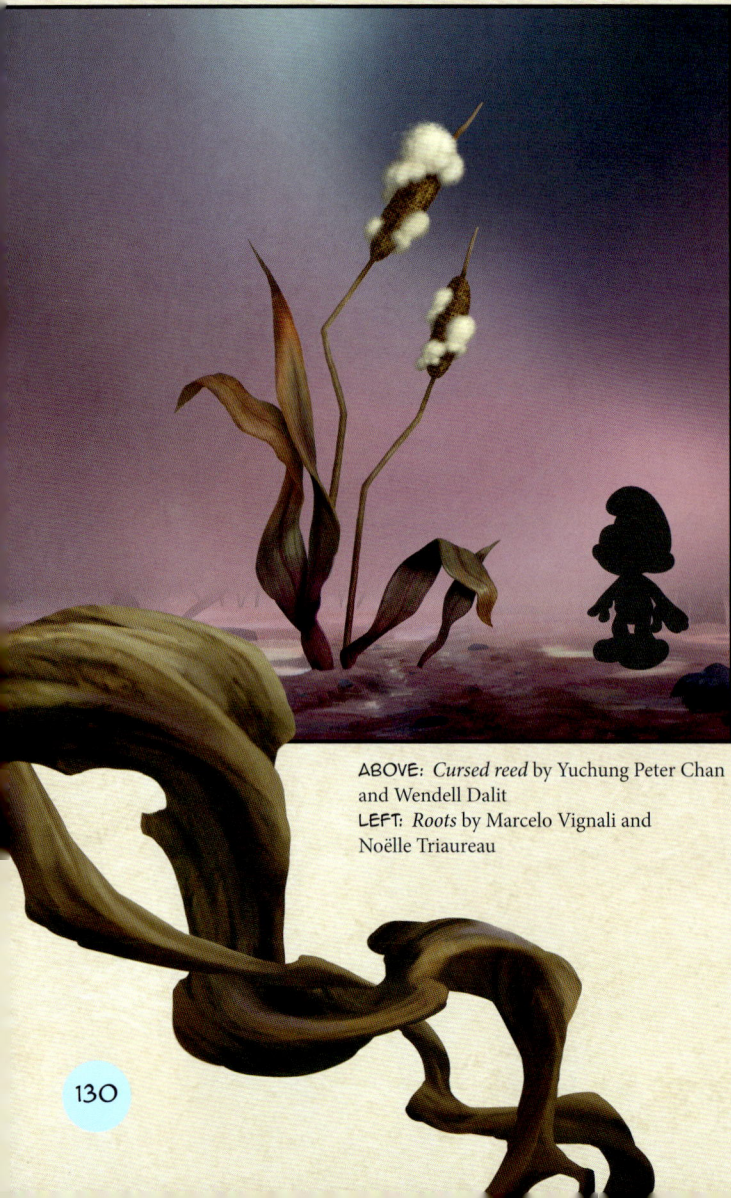

ABOVE: *Cursed reed* by Yuchung Peter Chan and Wendell Dalit
LEFT: *Roots* by Marcelo Vignali and Noëlle Triaureau

TOP: *Color key* by Noëlle Triaureau
MIDDLE: *Color key* by Jerry Loveland
ABOVE: *Color key* by Yuchung Peter Chan and Dean Gordon
RIGHT: *Three Tree Swamp* by Yuchung Peter Chan

130

ABOVE: *Three trees sketches* by Patrick Maté
BELOW: *Three Trees of Terror swamp* by Michael Spooner and Marcelo Vignali

PIRANHAS

"The swamp is intended to be more of a place for Gargamel to find himself in trouble, but in a comical way," notes director Kelly Asbury. Some of that comedy comes from his interaction with the aquatic life, namely the piranha-like fish. These might appear cute at first glance, but when these fish ruffle their scales and bare their teeth, they are not just smiling because they are happy to see visitors. "These fish were once multicolored like the palette of the Forbidden Forest, but now they are pure red to suggest their threatening nature," notes production designer Noëlle Triaureau.

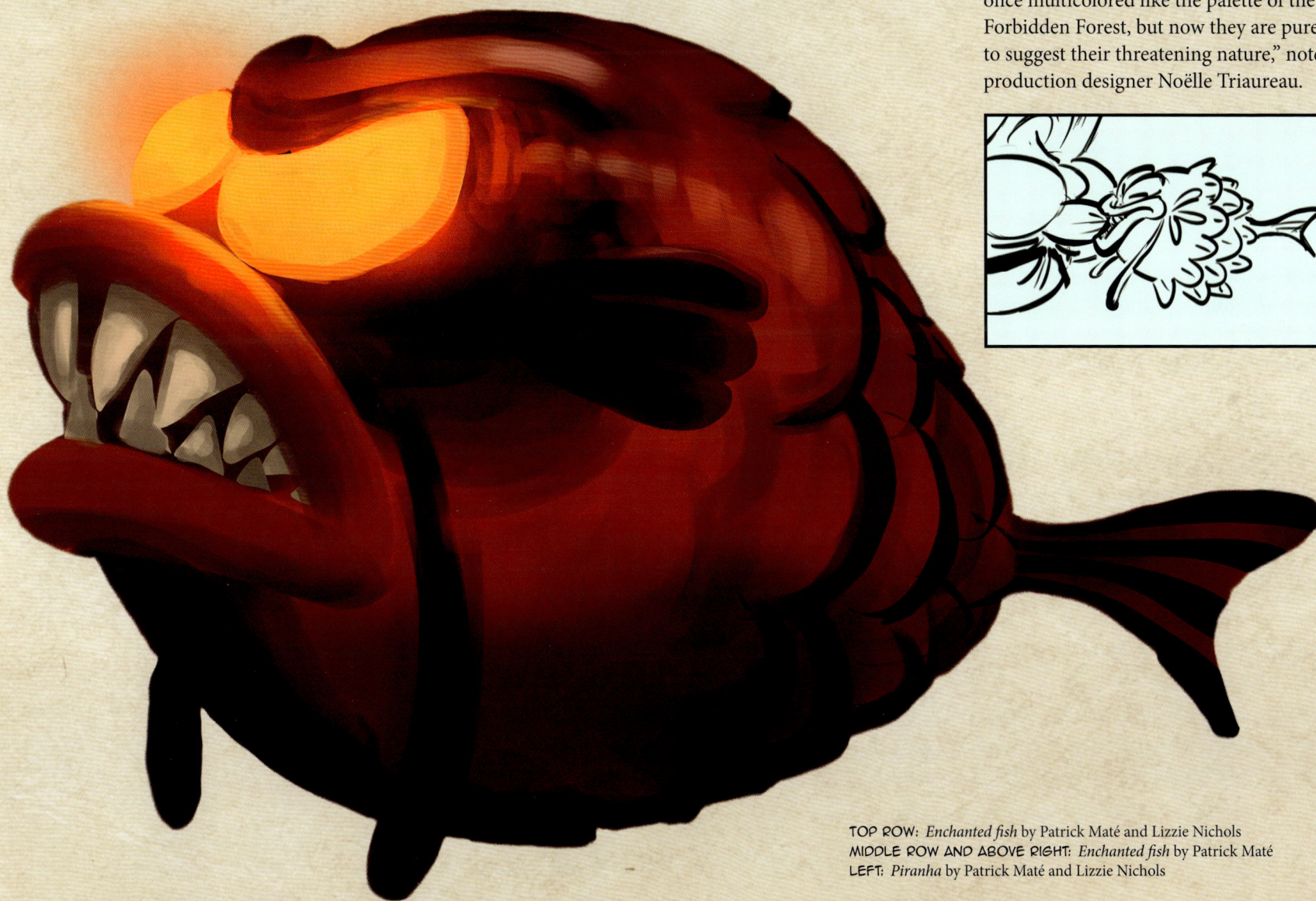

TOP ROW: *Enchanted fish* by Patrick Maté and Lizzie Nichols
MIDDLE ROW AND ABOVE RIGHT: *Enchanted fish* by Patrick Maté
LEFT: *Piranha* by Patrick Maté and Lizzie Nichols

133

-4-

WELCOME TO SMURFY GROVE

Behold, the most enchanting location in the forest is Smurfy Grove, home to yet another community of Smurfs. And if that is not exciting enough of a discovery, the fact that they are all female Smurfs is another level of surprise, especially for Smurfette.

The grove differs from Smurf Village in its color palette, even though both exist in forest settings. "The boy village is cast in yellows, and yellow green around the village; the girl grove is established with blue green and purples," explains production designer Noëlle Triaureau. Throughout the entire Smurf world, though, "we chose to saturate the colors along the lines of French impressionists—Monet, Degas, and such—never going too dark, but rather staying buoyant, beautiful, and appealing," adds director Kelly Asbury.

From a design perspective, the Smurfy Grove forest setting is home to very different foliage than what grows around Smurf Village. "Trees in the grove are larger, with roots that are long and twisted, which gives us an opportunity to create gnarly silhouettes and overlapping elements. They form an intricate maze of bridges, arches, walls, curves, half pipes, and tunnels for Smurfs to walk through," says Triaureau. Three central trees whose trunks are intertwined form the heart of the Smurf girl community, along with a stump that serves as their town square and is almost fortress-like in its security. "Having trees at the center of their community is an idea that dates back to our omnibus storyline, where he lived in a tree and Smurfs lived around him. Some ideas just feel so right that they continue on in the movie, when other details fall to the side," notes art director Marcelo Vignali.

As opposed to the boy homes that are grounded and housed in mushrooms, the girl homes are nest-like spheres, connected to branches up in the canopy of the trees. These truly are nests, woven out of twigs and leaves, first imagined by visual development artist Joty Lam as being on stilts and then carried upward into the canopy by Vignali.

PREVIOUS PAGES: *Smurfy Grove, girl village* by Noëlle Triaureau
RIGHT: *Smurfy Grove* by Marcelo Vignali and Dean Gordon
INSET: *Smurfy Grove* by Marcelo Vignali

ABOVE: *Storyboards* by Mike Kunkel

137

ABOVE: *Girl village* by Marcelo Vignali

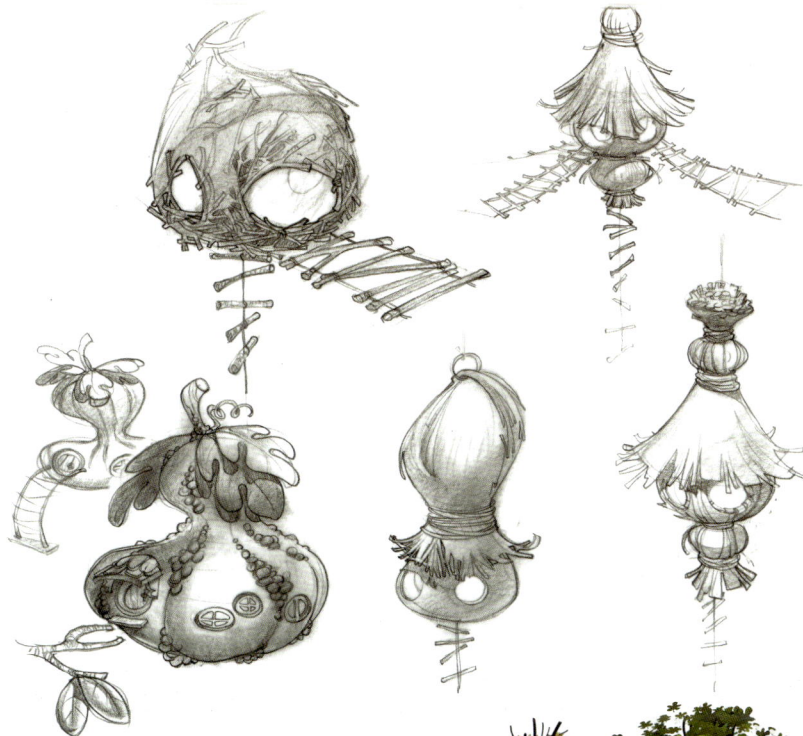

TOP AND TOP RIGHT: *Smurfy Grove homes* by Marcelo Vignali
ABOVE: *Smurfy Grove residents* by Patrick Maté
RIGHT: *Smurfy Grove house* by Marcelo Vignali and Naveen Selvanathan
FAR RIGHT: *Smurfy Grove* by Marcelo Vignali

MEET THE SMURF GIRLS

Adding new characters to a beloved legacy, let alone adding 99 of them, is a huge undertaking. Such a dynamic expansion of the world comes with great responsibility to chart a new path yet stay true to the universe of the Smurfs. "We were super mindful about the weight of this creative decision, since we knew it would change the franchise from here on out," recalls head of story Brandon Jeffords. But with thoughtful development between the team at Sony Pictures and the keepers of the Smurf lore, this journey of discovery led to a joyously creative place.

Having done his dissertation about women in comics, and how few there have been throughout history, character designer Patrick Maté was happy to add to their presence by creating the Smurf girls. "It seemed as if we were of the same mind as Peyo in creating the girl Smurfs, as after I shared my designs, Véronique showed us drawings her father had done but not shared widely, which were nearly identical," says Maté. "Patrick really captured the essence of Smurf in these characters, so much so that our design review with Véronique brought tears to her eyes, with her saying, 'These look just like designs my father did when he was alive, when he thought about making girls,'" recalls director Kelly Asbury.

To the delight of Peyo fans, a wonderful parallel between the reveal of Smurfs in the original comic and the introduction of Smurf girls in this film can be found in the forest . . . or, rather, in eyes peeking out from the forest. Peyo slowly teased the existence of Smurfs as they hid in bushes to spy on others in their presence. In homage to that momentous occasion, the Smurf girls mask themselves with gorgeous leafed disguises as they maneuver around and eventually approach the band of travelers in this story. "The girl Smurfs have been raised to live off the land and to

RIGHT: *Forest Smurfettes* by Patrick Maté and Dean Gordon
INSET: *Color key* by Wendell Dalit
OPPOSITE, TOP: *Storyboards* by Mike Kunkel
OPPOSITE, LEFT INSET: *Color key* by Wendell Dalit and Noëlle Triaureau
OPPOSITE, RIGHT INSET: *Color key* by Wendell Dalit

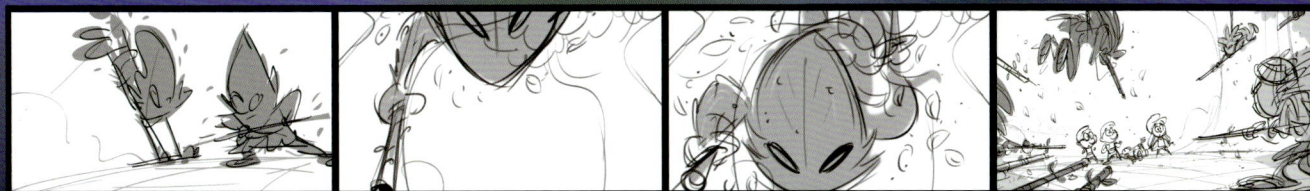

The girls' camouflage outfits are designed so that they can blend in the Forbidden Forest foliage. We cannot tell that they are Smurfs: even their arms and legs are covered with a type of clay that hides the blue of their skin.

— NOËLLE TRIAUREAU,
Production Designer

become one with it. It's only fitting that they use the very foliage as a means of protecting themselves. They are of nature," adds Asbury. Once the Smurf girls step out from behind their camouflage, they welcome Smurfette and her fellow traveling companions into their world, and into a whole new mind-set.

The social structure in the Smurf girls' community is different, with names that are not defined by strengths or weaknesses or talents, as is characteristic in the boys' village. "We had thought about creating a mirror world, but the keepers of the Smurf legacy steered us away from that," says Jeffords. "Véronique did not want to replicate the notion that everyone has one defining quality," adds Kristine Belson, president of Sony Pictures Animation. Writer Pam Ribon took that directive and developed it into a story point: Smurfette could not figure herself out in a community wherein her name does not define her role like the others, so when she arrived in Smurfy Grove and asked, "How do you know what you do or are?" she finally found the answer. "Smurfette sees that the girls do all kinds of diverse things and are not limited by their names. It's a whole new cultural philosophy for her, realizing that you can be whatever you want to be and don't have to have a label," explains Asbury. Smurfette and the audience soon discover that the members of the Smurf girl community are strong examples of individuality within a new societal concept, regardless of their inherent anatomical similarities.

141

SMURFSTORM, SMURFBLOSSOM & SMURFLILY

A trio of Smurf girls takes the lead in welcoming Smurfette and her fellow travelers to their community. Like Smurfwillow, their names reflect their environment instead of a particular characteristic, and each exhibits the independent thinking and unique persona that Smurfwillow has lovingly fostered in her culture. "The Smurf girls are even closer to nature than the boys. They use camouflage to keep themselves safe. For this reason their dress and hat are a sand color instead of white. Their clothing and accessories are made of and look like plants and flowers," explains character designer Patrick Maté.

Smurfstorm is a Smurf of few words but great presence, conveying a quiet, reserved confidence that adds power to her physical strength and agility. "She's tough, clearly a warrior at heart," says producer Jordan Kerner.

Smurfblossom provides counterbalance to the strong but silent type, since she is "full of energy and bouncing all over the place," says animation supervisor Alan Hawkins.

Smurflily is a bit more of an introvert, portraying more intelligence than physical power, yet is ready to participate in whatever the community needs.

TOP AND ABOVE: *Smurfstorm poses* by Patrick Maté
RIGHT: *Smurfstorm, final character render*

TOP LEFT, TOP MIDDLE, AND TOP FAR RIGHT:
Forest Smurfettes by Patrick Maté
RIGHT: *Smurflily, final character render*
LEFT: *Smurfblossom, final character render*
BELOW: *Costume variations by Patrick Maté*

SMURFWILLOW

Leading the community of Smurf girls is Smurfwillow, marked with authority by her white hair and red clothing, similar to Papa Smurf. Although she plays a role comparable to that of Papa Smurf, she is not called Mama Smurf because she is meant to be more of a grande dame than a matriarch. (Papa Smurf is only referred to as "Papa" in English, and his name is interpreted along the less paternal lines of "Great Smurf" or "Grand Smurf" in every other language.) Smurfwillow "carries herself very confidently, with reserved, thoughtful expressions and controlled timing," notes animation supervisor Alan Hawkins.

Papa Smurf and Smurfwillow have each been the only leader in their respective lives, so when they meet one another, they start to jockey for who is the true leader in a good-humored way. Clearly they have established their communities based on very different principles—his is about being defined by a leading characteristic or talent, and hers is about being an independent creature defined by what she enjoys on her own terms. But both are still revered and looked to for advice in their community.

Earlier versions of the story dug into the Smurf origins a bit deeper and played out that her name was Sigrid and she had a field of bluebells near Papa/Pieter's mushroom farm, with a bit of a love story woven into their tale.

ABOVE: *Color key* by Noëlle Triaureau
RIGHT: *Smurfwillow* by Patrick Maté and Kristy Kay

144

THIS PAGE: *Smurfwillow character poses* by Patrick Maté

145

ABOVE: *Smurfy Grove exploration* by Marcelo Vignali
ABOVE RIGHT: *Smurfwillow house exterior* by
Marcelo Vignali and Kristy Kay
BELOW: *Smurfwillow house*
by Marcelo Vignali and
Dean Gordon

TOP AND MIDDLE LEFT:
Smurfwillow by Patrick Maté
LEFT AND RIGHT: *Smurfwillow,
final character renders*

147

OTHER SMURFY GROVE RESIDENTS

To come up with 99 Smurf girls, and to follow the Peyo tradition of using the same base to create individual characters, "all of the Smurf girls are unique but based on the Smurfette model. We played with heights, proportions, and accessories to give them their own distinct looks," explains head of modeling Marvin Kim. Specifically, the variations are built with one Smurf girl model; nine hairstyles with bangs that turn on and off to make 18 different looks; three types of dresses, with or without vests; a number of accessories including jewelry and a variety of flowers for their hair; and two shoe options.

"We may not need to worry about varying skin tone or eye color on these variants, but they all require hair and cloth simulation, which adds to their complexity," notes visual effects supervisor Mike Ford. Since the top of the head or hair remains hidden in Smurf tradition, except for Smurfette and Papa, it was interesting for the team to style hair for the girls that felt right, with so little reference to consider. After exploring a variety of styles and colors, the artistic team chose "hairstyles that are pretty workable and symmetrical, with no flips like Smurfette wears," says animation supervisor Alan Hawkins.

The Smurf girls may all be rather independent creatures, but they work well together to fulfill the needs of their community, and sometimes they even combine efforts with their natural neighbors, including butterflies, caterpillars, and spiders, to get the job done.

ABOVE: *Forest Smurfettes* by Patrick Maté
RIGHT: *Forest Smurfettes* by Patrick Maté

Smurfette reacts in amazement to the discovery that other girls exist. She calls theirs a "lost village," but they think, "We weren't lost, you were!"

— KRISTINE BELSON,
President of Sony Pictures Animation

THIS PAGE AND OPPOSITE, MIDDLE AND BOTTOM:
Forest Smurfettes by Patrick Maté
OPPOSITE, TOP: *Forest Smurfette expressions* by Patrick Maté

With the way he brought the Smurf girls into our world, it is clear that Patrick Maté has mastered the Peyo look.

— KELLY ASBURY
Director

Living in the Forbidden Forest, the Smurf girls evolved into resourceful beings, capable of camouflaging and protecting themselves like warriors.

— NOËLLE TRIAUREAU,
Production Designer

THIS PAGE: *Forest Smurfs camouflage explorations by Yuchung Peter Chan*

THIS PAGE: *Smurfy Grove attacks!*
by Patrick Maté

153

THE END OF THE JOURNEY

Long ago, Peyo gave the Smurfs a motto—"Together we are stronger"—and this certainly rings true in *Smurfs: The Lost Village*. On screen, Smurfette feels it as she encounters a whole new community and culture of Smurfs, which, in turn, supports her in her journey of self-discovery. Behind the screen, director Kelly Asbury attests to the fact that "a director is only as good as his team—it really is a component of different people doing what they do and me allowing them to do it. I have a huge wonderful team of colleagues, and I give them every bit of credit for making this come together. It takes a Smurf village."

Indeed, the cinematic journey that has brought Peyo's vision together with Sony Picture's animation talent joyfully perpetuates the magic of Smurfs to future generations, making their ever-blue presence even stronger.

RIGHT: *Smurfette, final character render*
BELOW: *Color key* by Sean Eckols
OPPOSITE: *Smurfy Grove* by Kristy Kay
FOLLOWING PAGES: *Forbidden Forest* by Noëlle Triaureau

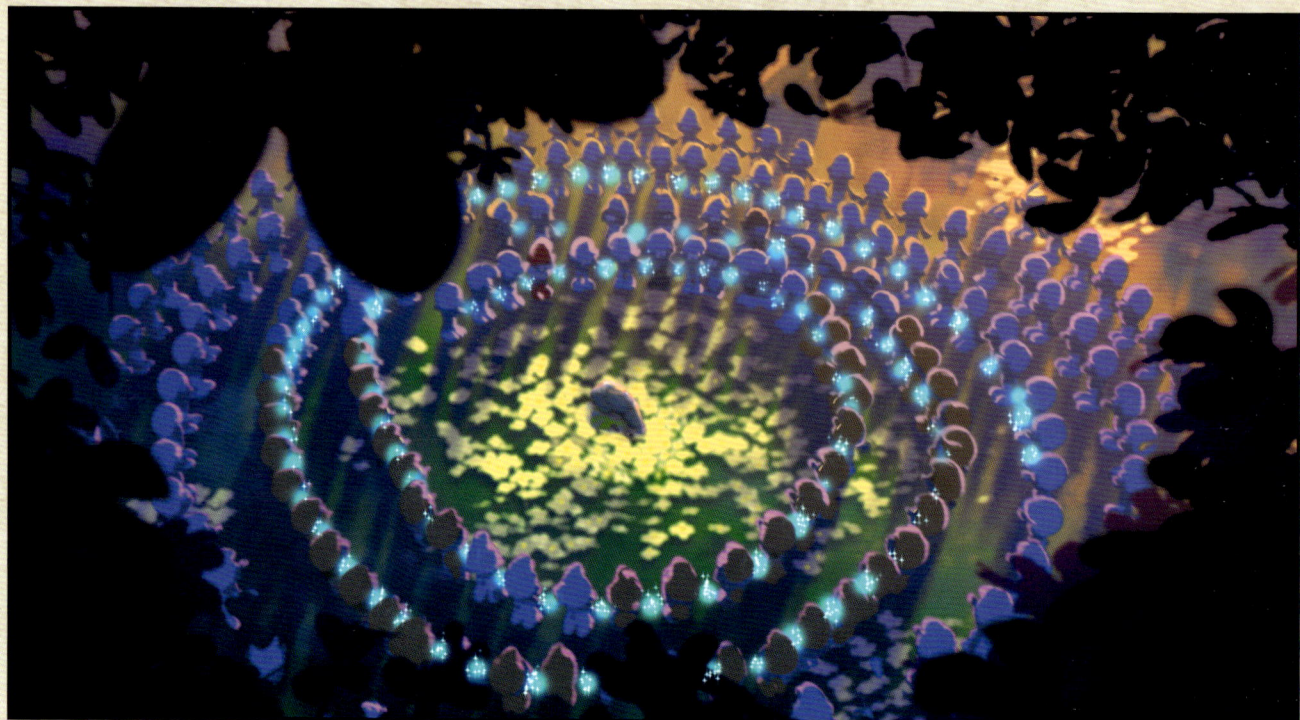

ABOVE: *Storyboards* by Denise Koyama

ACKNOWLEDGMENTS

I am thankful for the true-blue support of the folks at Sony Pictures Animation, particularly Melissa Sturm, Virginia King, and Kristine Belson, without whom this book would not exist. I deeply appreciate the entire creative community at SPA, which gathered to create this film and somehow also found time to welcome me into their busy schedule . . . you are all Smurftastic! I am always thrilled to partner with the gang at Cameron + Company as well, especially the amazing Iain Morris.

Last but not least, I am ever grateful for my own village of family and friends, and for the joy of life that we share each and every day, even if we don't live together in a Forbidden Forest.

TRACEY MILLER-ZARNEKE

TEAM SMURF

VISUAL DEVELOPMENT TEAM

STORY, EDITORIAL AND FRONT END PRODUCTION TEAMS

IMAGEWORKS SHOT PRODUCTION CREW – VANCOUVER

IMAGEWORKS SHOT PRODUCTION CREW – CULVER CITY

COLOPHON

Published by arrangement CAMERON + COMPANY
6 Petaluma Blvd. North, Suite B6, Petaluma, CA 94952

www.cameronbooks.com

PUBLISHER: Chris Gruener
CREATIVE DIRECTOR: Iain R. Morris
DESIGNER: Barbara Genetin
MANAGING EDITOR: Jan Hughes
COPY EDITOR: Judith Dunham

A CIP catalogue record for this title is available from the British Library.

ISBN: 9781785655326 • 10 9 8 7 6 5 4 3 2 1 • Printed and bound in China

Published in the UK and Australia by Titan Books in 2017.

TITAN BOOKS

A division of Titan Publishing Group Ltd
144 Southwark Street, London SE1 0UP
www.titanbooks.com

CAMERON + COMPANY would like to thank Tracey-Miller Zarneke for telling the behind-the-scenes story of *Smurfs: The Lost Village* with such insight and vitality; Iain Morris for his always-spot-on art direction and design; Barbara Genetin for her assistance with design; Mark Voss for initial design help; Judith Dunham, in whose hands we always trust our copy; Virginia King and Sony Pictures Consumer Products; Melissa Sturm, and everyone at Sony Pictures Animation for the honor and pleasure of publishing this book.

THIS PAGE, BACKGROUND: *Forest adventure* by Joty Lam
ABOVE: *Clown Smurf* by Patrick Maté
FRONT ENDPAPERS: *Papa's lab* by Marcelo Vignali and Dean Gordon
BACK ENDPAPERS: *Forbidden Forest* by Wendell Dalit
COVER: *Dragonfly rider* by Noëlle Triaureau
BACK COVER INSET, TOP: *Smurfy Grove exploration* by Marcelo Vignali